THE FREELANCER'S COMPASS

THE FREELANCER'S COMPASS

Navigate Your Way from Corporate Cog to Solopreneur Star

RODIKA TOLLEFSON

[100% human-produced]

Audacia Press
PO Box 848
Shelton, WA 98584
USA

Ordering Information:
Quantity sales. Special discounts are available on quantity purchases by corporations, associations, and others. For details, contact the "Special Sales Department" at the address above.

The Freelancer's Compass/Rodika Tollefson — 1st ed.

ISBN: 979-8-9908047-1-5

Cover design by Lucy Arnold | lucyarnold.com

For Darrin, whose moral support and friendship
have helped me weather the ups and downs.

And for Diane and Mary, my patient and
inspiring peer mentors, sounding board VIPs, and
"tell-it-like-it-is" accountability buddies without
whom I would be very likely lost. Every
solopreneur needs a Diane and Mary in their life.

Contents

Introduction

I f you've been mulling over the idea of jumping the corporate ship into the wide ocean of freelancing, you'll find plenty of content on launching a business or freelance career. This book is not that, or at least not exactly.

The Freelancer's Compass is intended for those who want more precise rather than generic guidance on how to go from being a cog in the corporate machine to serving as an independent consultant. More specifically, this book will guide you in setting yourself up for success from the start so you can deliberately grow your business rather than allowing it to simply "happen."

Most of my advice applies to any type of knowledge and consulting work. But I'm speaking directly to you, marketing professionals, for two reasons. One, because you are my peeps. And two, because our industry has been going through a rough time and many corporate professionals are looking for alternatives.

For the past four or five years, my marketing and communications business has been going gangbusters. I could barely keep up with demand, working 40-plus hours a week just on client deliverables.

But more recently, I experienced the same thing as many other content marketing writers and copywriters in the technology and cybersecurity sectors did: a noticeable drop in inbound leads and projects from existing customers. If you're a marketer in tech or any number of other sectors, you may have felt the pinch yourself. Perhaps your team was downsized and you were swept in the process — which is why you're here.

Since I had to scurry to replace a few projects that dropped off, I tried an old trick that worked a few years back: I searched for freelance gigs on LinkedIn.

Except the hashtags that in the past produced potential leads (e.g., #freelance writer, #hiring copywriter) now surfaced post after post from content marketing writers, strategists, and managers who had lost their jobs. They were updating their network that they were #open for work. Any work, even #freelance.

Those posts were the inspiration for this book.

The worlds of corporate employees and freelancers are miles apart, even if they are producing the same deliverable. Imagine flying your own two-seat "puddle jumper" instead of taking a commercial flight. You'll reach the same destination, but how you get there is a completely different experience.

I know this because I've been in business for myself for about 25 years, and I was once embedded for 10 months with a product marketing team at a Fortune 100 tech company as a full-time contracted writer. Same end product, generally speaking. Two totally different trips.

You already know how to be awesome at your job. My goal is to help you rock the other part of being a freelancer — the nitty-gritty, behind-the-scenes stuff you have to do as a business owner.

And let's be clear: If you've taken the freelance road, even if as a stopgap, you are a business owner.

Welcome to the roller coaster! It may get thrilling and terrifying at the same time, so buckle up.

PART I

Getting Into the Right Mindset

In Part I, we look at the differences between employment and self-employment and the mindset shift that will help you make a successful transition from one to the other.

Chapter 1

From Corporate Cog to a Team of One

"Courage is the power to let go of the familiar."

— *Raymond Lindquist*

When you "worked for the man," you may have envied your freelance colleagues, fantasizing about being your own boss.

Working in pajamas? Escaping the hellacious loop of back-to-back meetings? Swapping the daily rush-hour traffic for a 10-second "commute"? That's the life!

During the pandemic, flexibility became the corporate mantra, and every day was casual Friday at best. So, most people got a taste of what it's like to crawl out of bed and roll straight into the "office" wearing their stretchy pants. But even during those times when Smokey and Rover were your only office mates — and you played Coffitivity just so you could "feel" the office vibe — your team, your manager, your go-to co-workers were just one Slack room, Teams chat, or Zoom call away.

If you've only worked in a corporate environment before, freelancing may be a cultural shock.

Sure, there are tons of perks besides the freedom over which projects to take on. No more weekly syncs with your manager. No more wasted time on "all-hands." No more fretting over your pending PTO request so you can attend cousin Betty's wedding.

It all sounds wonderful — and it is.

But making the leap also means leaving behind a wealth of resources (human and other) that you probably took for granted.

Whether your team worked together like clockwork or was a hot mess, you were merely a cog in the corporate machine. Someone else had to worry about setting up your email account, paying for the corporate apps you used, troubleshooting your computer, invoicing customers, maintaining the website, tracking financials, selling your company's widgets, and so on.

As a freelancer, you're not a cog. You're the gear, pinion, axis, and whatever other doohickey it takes for the entire mechanism to function. And the gearhead who designs and makes it all work.

When you're first starting out, you're the IT help desk, accounting clerk, admin assistant, webmaster, marketing director, salesperson, project manager, customer success rep, and service provider all at once. Welcome to freedom!

If a machine is missing a cog or two, it won't grind to a halt. But it will certainly not function well.

Your freelance machine has a lot of moving parts beyond deliverables. Hence, my focus is on operations — the less glamorous part of the freelance life that many people ignore for too long. (Yes, I was one of those people.)

During the Great Resignation, numerous corporate cogs left to build their own freelance machine — one with shiny-new parts that were well-oiled and maintenance-free. Many gave up a few short months later, realizing there's nothing "free" in freelance, maintenance or otherwise.

When they came down from the high of their daring escape, these daredevils realized that going solo took a lot more than proficiency and skill in their job.

Making the successful transition to a team of one means setting up business processes, implementing tools, creating habits, building a network, and taking other necessary steps that help you grow into a resilient and thriving freelancer.

I wrote this book to teach you the ropes of making that transition. To help you stop thinking of yourself as a freelancer and start acting like a business owner.

If you were successful in your job, you can do the same in your business — with a little mindset adjustment and some systems in place.

Who Am I to Give You Advice?

TL; DR After getting my first journalism job (as a beat reporter for a weekly newspaper) following j-school graduation, I quit 10 months later for the "freedom" of freelance life. Since then, I've run a writing business for 25 years, freelancing full-time for most of it (with two detours of having a "real job" and freelancing on the side).

I've grown my company to a six-figure income while having the pleasure of working with some of the world's biggest companies, as well as numerous startups, small businesses, and even government agencies and nonprofits.

The long version: I traded the "stability" of a paycheck after figuring out that the job of a reporter didn't play nice with the job of a mother to two very young kids. I needed the flexibility to make my own schedule. Little did I know about the "feast or famine" that's inherent with freelancing (if you're not planning mindfully) or about the other costs of self-employment.

I've dabbled a few times since then with the idea of getting a full-time job with perks like paid vacation and sick leave, medical insurance, and a stable paycheck. But I have not gone back to "punching the clock" — save for the two times when I couldn't pass up an incredible career-building opportunity in exchange for having an actual boss.

Once you've learned how to run your own business in a fulfilling way and be the captain of your own ship, it's tough to go back.

Along the way, I've made a ton of mistakes. (For example, I didn't consistently require written agreements or deposits for almost two decades — go ahead, judge me.) But I've learned from them. And I still learn every day how to run my business better, how to deliver better services, how to implement new systems that can help me level up.

I've worked directly with clients like Dell Technologies, American Express, Cisco, Dashlane, Proofpoint, and Kaspersky. I've also delivered projects for companies like Lenovo, Microsoft, STANLEY, Samsung, and CVS through marketing or content agencies.

Getting there — and breaking six figures — was a long road. But it would have been a lot shorter and a lot less frustrating if I had put in place sooner the strategies and essential business systems that I'm sharing with you.

In addition to my own experience, I include short profiles of successful solopreneurs throughout the book. These pros share their insights into their challenges and triumphs — and offer valuable lessons for us all.

First, a Disclaimer or Three

1. I'm not a lawyer or an accountant.

Throughout the book, I talk about various things that have financial and legal implications, like taxes and liability. I am not an attorney, a certified public accountant (CPA), or any other type of professional you should consult for financial, legal, or other professional advice.

I am simply sharing what I know — and I don't claim to know everything there is to know about running a freelance business. I work with a CPA and a business lawyer when making decisions that affect the success and resilience of my company, and I strongly urge you to do the same. (I provide a few ideas in Chapter 8 for where to get free help when you're first starting out.)

2. Results may vary.

Just like it says in the tiny print you see in ads for self-improvement or business development programs, my experience is not necessarily the same as others. I am part of an extensive network of freelancers/business owners who share their experiences, advice, and intel with each other, and a lot of the practices I describe in this book are standard.

That said, we all have our own ways of doing business, and what works for one person may not work for others. Take my advice as a starting point for doing your due diligence, not as gospel. Just like adopting a healthy lifestyle entails reading a lot of (often contradicting) research and advice, then creating your own mash-up that works best for you, running a business means inhaling as much information as you can, considering the best advice that makes sense to you, and then creating your own business model to fit your vision and goals.

3. Don't expect the moon and the sky.

There are plenty of books about growing your business, breaking six figures, creating a niche, marketing, finding potential clients, diversifying your income, and so forth. This book talks about none of those things in detail, if at all.

My goal is to help you understand the difference between a solopreneur and an employee, the fundamentals that ensure your business is legit and professional, and various other aspects that many of us dread and some may be willing to give our left arm for if those responsibilities would just go away.

Chapter 2

You Are a Business Owner, not a Freelancer

Attitude is a little thing that makes a big difference."

— *Winston Churchill*

I f you plunged into this adventure in a hurry, going freelance as a necessity rather than as a lifestyle or career choice, you likely moved fast to find a client — any client — and then focused all your time and energy on delivering and on finding the next project.

Bringing in the money is certainly the main point of this endeavor, so it stands to reason you started there.

But at some point, preferably sooner rather than later, you need to ask yourself: Is this a stopgap play for a couple of months while I find a new full-time job? Or is self-employment my new career path?

If you're thinking "in and out," you should stop reading this book and do something more productive, like binge-watching *The Mandalorian* or *Ozark*.

If, however, you are in this for the duration and want to ensure long-term success, you won't get there by moving haphazardly from one project to the next. You need to be a professional, and that doesn't mean just producing a quality final product.

Clients may question your choices if you do business via Gmail (or worse, Yahoo), but they don't care (with some exceptions) whether you have a business license, a project management app, or a paid Zoom plan.

Can you deliver on your projects without all those things? Of course.

Will you still be here tomorrow without a professional website, a client onboarding process, a marketing plan, and jargony-sounding tools like standard operating procedures (SOPs)? Probably.

Will you be able to make a consistent living year after year without all those things (and more)? Only if you're very lucky — or perhaps if you're very good at sales or have an incredible referral network.

Do you want to avoid taking the scenic route or going on a roller-coaster ride and instead build a strong freelance career faster?

Don't think of yourself as a gig worker, the hired hand who takes whatever work comes along because … bills. Stop thinking like a project-by-project freelancer and start thinking like the CEO of your own company.

A successful business needs four fundamental things (to start with):

- **Infrastructure:** Proper business structure, contracts, and other legal mumbo jumbo that keeps our lawyers in business.

- **Processes:** Onboarding checklists, client management SOPs, project delivery workflows, and other boring stuff that most people hate thinking about unless they're some sort of freak.

- **Tools and support systems:** Bookkeeping, scheduling, and other apps; backup and data security systems; virtual assistants (VAs) — eventually; and other things that make your life easier and keep your fingernails intact.

- **A roadmap:** You're not Microsoft; you don't need an elaborate document filled with business-speak and fancy charts — maybe just a two-page business plan that states your goals, vision, revenue objectives, customer acquisition strategies, and a few other basics that may make you yawn, yet will help keep you focused.

All this may sound overwhelming enough to make you want to update your resume and post it on indeed.com.

Chillax.

You don't need all of these things in place — or possibly any of them — before you toggle the "Open to Work" button on LinkedIn.

You can get all your ducks in a row gradually, step by step. We'll cover each of these fundamentals in the following chapters, and I'll help you prioritize them as well.

Just don't put it off for too long because I guarantee that, eventually, you'll run into problems.

To borrow from corporate-speak again, you need to mitigate your risks (which could be anything from nonpaying customers and scope creep to a dry pipeline and an enormous end-of-year tax bill). The best way to do that is through prevention (hence infrastructure, processes, yada-yada).

Freelancer vs. Business Owner: What Does the Mindset Look Like?

Freelancers	Business owners/ entrepreneurs
- Drift from one project to the next, letting business happen as it comes.	- Have a long-term vision and goals, and a strategy to get there.
- Allow their clients to dictate the price or underprice themselves consistently.	- Set fees based on an understanding of the market, their value, and clients' objectives.
- Describe themselves or their work in terms of deliverables (e.g., content types/formats).	- Describe themselves or their work in terms of results and solutions to clients' problems.
- Have no idea what to say or have inconsistent answers when a prospect asks, "How do you work with clients?"	- Have a clear idea of their business model, client management process, workflow, etc.
- Take any project available as long as the money looks reasonable.	- Have a thought-out checklist for what makes a project a good fit and turn down anything that doesn't check off at least some of the boxes.

Three Main Reasons to Think Like an Entrepreneur

1. If you don't take yourself seriously, no one else will.

And you're not taking yourself seriously if you wing your processes — and, one might argue, if your business email ends with gmail.com.

2. You're here for the same reason as any business: to make money.

You're not dabbling or looking for a hobby that simply pays for itself. As a business owner, you'll do what you must to stay profitable.

3. You can detach from your company.

Which means you learn not to take things personally. You can even "hide" behind your processes. ("Sorry [not sorry], dear client; it's simply how I do business.")

The business mindset also helps you become comfortable setting the rates that you need to be profitable, negotiating terms with clients, standing your ground when something goes south, and navigating other dicey situations that you may not love.

When you don't take your business dealings personally, it's easier to say things like:

- "The rates are the rates." [This is not a garage sale or a bulk-discount store.]

- "No, I can't start this project until we agree on the scope and fee and I receive the deposit." [You don't tell your lawyer, accountant, or dentist that you'll check the work first and then decide if you'll pay and how much; why would you ask me to?]

- "Sure, I can put a rush on this — for an X fee." [I really like you, but my business can't survive on favors.]

Three Myths About the Self-Employment Life

1. You can do what you want.

True, you are your own boss.

No one can tell you how or where to work.

You can choose or decline any project. Work from the beach, your couch, your neighborhood pub, or a villa in Italy. Only take meetings on Tuesdays. Refuse to deliver in Google Docs (that may be just me). You get the idea.

In reality, you may not be in a position to decline projects that aren't a great fit, at least while you get started and begin filling your pipeline consistently.

Although you have your own process, you may have to follow the clients' workflows instead — even use their preferred apps. (Really, what's wrong with Microsoft Word?)

And, instead of being accountable to one person — your manager — you are now accountable to several clients all at once. They have competing priorities and deadlines, and it's up to you to manage your workload to meet them all.

2. You have a flexible schedule.

Of course it's flexible! Work at 3 a.m. or 8 p.m. Work just one hour a day and then cram for 12 before your deadline — nobody cares as long as you deliver high-quality work on time.

So long, vacation requests at the mercy of HR or your boss! Take as much time off as you'd like, whenever you want.

In reality, you're at the whim of your client deadlines.

You may have to work evenings, weekends, and very long weeks. You may need to schedule your vacation around recurring deadline cycles, plan time off far in advance, and cancel a weekend getaway at the last minute.

If you want to avoid these kinds of scenarios, you'll need to:

- Set your boundaries. (If working at all hours, all the time, is a deal-breaker, you will have to rethink how many projects you take and when.)

- Understand your priorities (Family time? Paying the mortgage? Getting R&R to stay sane?) and know your nonnegotiables when setting and managing client expectations.

Plus, without a steady paycheck (or a boss) to compel you to show up every day, you have to motivate yourself to keep going and work on your business even if you don't have a client deadline.

3. "Feast or famine" is the way of life.

Feast or famine is real.

Even after many years in business, I was not a complete stranger to this side effect of living the freelance dream. I can't tell you how many times I got a phone call or email informing me that a project I'd done for years was moved in-house or defunded, or an ongoing monthly project was canceled without any notice — sometimes more than one project in the same month.

It's not easy, but you can avoid the feast-or-famine cycle. It takes consistent marketing, diversification, planning, and other strategies.

Although these aspects are beyond the scope of this book, I bring up this myth because it's a lot harder to break the feast-or-famine cycle without having your infrastructure and processes in place.

Three Simple Ways to Show Up for Your Business Every Workday

Forget all the paperwork and other back-end minutia for a moment. You can show you're serious about your business by taking three simple actions.

1. Set up office hours.

I am not a morning person, so I start my workday at 9 a.m. Monday–Friday, and I rarely quit before 5 or 6 p.m. I make case-by-case exceptions for occasional client meetings before 9, a byproduct of living on the West Coast and working with clients all over the world.

(If we have a good relationship, my clients know better because I advertise, as necessary, that I have no working brain before 8:30 a.m.)

If I don't get to my office at 9 a.m., I often lament that I'm late. Who cares? I do.

I am not doing this to prove anything to anyone.

I do it because signing my own paycheck doesn't mean showing up whenever I'm good and ready. (I may never be good and ready on some days.)

Am I always working 9–5 straight? Of course not; I'm not a robot or a monster boss.

I have places to drive people to, medical appointments to keep, and a gym membership to use. Several times a week, one of my sons and I take 20-minute coffee breaks together. (He makes the espresso; need I say more?) Sometimes those 20 minutes may even stretch beyond an hour.

Occasionally, if I don't have a pressing deadline, I'll take a few hours off in the middle of the day on Thursday or Friday to go to lunch or thrift shopping for my art hobby.

Some weeks, I quit early on Friday to go on a date with my husband or to my Happy Place (my art studio, formerly known as the master bedroom's second walk-in closet) — usually as a reward to myself for a tough week or maybe 10- to 12-hour workdays.

Unless it's truly a slow time (which hasn't been the case for years except for a temporary recent lull), I know I'll have to make up the missed time on a weekend or in the evening. Most likely both.

And I'm good with that. Flexibility, after all, is one of the reasons I run my own show.

Even on my slowest weeks, I don't put in fewer than 30 hours. I take advantage of the downtime to learn new things, catch up on marketing and admin, or brainstorm ideas for growing the business.

All this to say: Figure out when your most productive hours start, whether that's 6 a.m. or 1 p.m., and how many days and hours you need to work each day to earn what you want to earn (plus do the requisite businessy things).

Make those your office hours.

Show up on time regardless of whether you have a client project or deadline. You have plenty of other things to do. Leave early if you are completely spent or just want to give yourself a break, but don't make it a daily habit.

You may be your own boss, but that doesn't mean you're not accountable to yourself.

This is your job, no matter that you're signing your own paycheck.

Keep in mind that you may have to bend your office hours to chat with a client, attend a prospect meeting, meet a deadline rush, or tend to a family obligation.

But, unless you have a big time difference with your client or there's another extenuating circumstance, you can absolutely make yourself unavailable outside of office hours.

Simply tell your client at the beginning of your relationship that, with few exceptions, you only schedule meetings at X times or on X days so you can do deep work the rest of the week.

Nobody needs to know that your deep work may involve shopping at Pottery Barn, planting tomatoes, or watching *The Office*, *Silicon Valley*, or *Suits* to remind yourself why you quit the corporate life.

Pro Tip

You'll need a phone number for your business. (I can't believe it either, but some people will call rather than email.)

Whatever you choose, don't use your home number, especially if you have young kids. You don't want little Johnny or Susie answering your "business" line when a prospect or client calls out of the blue.

Many people use their mobile number. This is fine, but you'll end up disclosing that number (on your website, for example, or when you sign up for some gated asset for research) — so be prepared for B2B sales calls on your personal cell. If you're like me, you don't answer random calls. Still, annoying.

You can, of course, get a free Google number so you don't have to give out your cell number. But those calls ring on your personal mobile line, so what's the point?

2. Ditch the PJs. Seriously.

I won't lie, I've rolled into my office in my pajamas straight out of bed plenty of times.

When my office was right next to my bedroom, I was happy to go from bed to desk in 10 seconds flat. I was comfortable and in a hurry, and I didn't care. I was also not making very much money while regularly working 50-hour weeks.

Those days are long gone.

I still wear comfortable clothing, but I have an office "dress code." No PJs. No sweatpants. No stained, torn, or plain T-shirts. No looking like I just rolled out of bed or am getting ready to work out.

I buy clothes specifically for work, and (most times) these are clothes that I wouldn't be embarrassed to wear in public.

Again, who cares what you wear? Nobody.

After all, Zoom or Teams won't betray your poor wardrobe choices unless you wear something completely inappropriate. (But just in case, double-check how you look on camera before you join meetings.)

I wear casual but designated work clothes not because I need to be ready to make a run for it at all times. Or because my client interactions require "office attire." I do it because I'm a professional who comes to the office to do a job, not to lounge around.

I finally realized, after a few years in business, that dressing up to come to work completely changed my attitude.

Sure, jeans or comfy pants with a stylish T-shirt or casual button-down shirt are not much of a "dressing up." But it works for me as the cue that I'm entering the headspace where I focus and get things done.

And yes, I make a lot more money now than I did in those pajama days. A buttload more. A wardrobe makeover was only a small part of it, but it was certainly the spark that started me on the path to treating my business seriously instead of letting the work happen to me.

Whatever your version of casual office attire is, take a little time to decide your dress code. Even if they're tees and designer sweats, only wear those clothes to work and not on your time off, just like you would if you worked in a corporate office.

I promise you, once you ditch the loungewear and stop commingling your work and play clothing, you'll feel differently about your workday. It's a very subtle mindset shift, but enough to make you much more productive.

Pro Tip

When you have an extra $25–$50 and a business logo, buy yourself a T-shirt or two with the logo on it. Wear those on video calls with prospects, especially if it's Friday (as in, casual Friday).

If your prospect is observant, the T may become a conversation starter or a memorable detail about you. At the very least, it may impress them that you've spent money on your company bling, even if they don't say it out loud.

3. Designate an office space.

There's absolutely nothing wrong with working at your kitchen counter, at the dining table, or on the living room couch. Especially if all you need is a laptop and Wi-Fi.

But there are a few problems with this setup if you're planning to work for yourself for the long haul.

You know how sleep experts say you shouldn't have a TV in your bedroom? The idea is to use that space for winding down and sleeping.

Most of us ignore these recommendations (raise your hand if you have a bedroom TV like me), but there's a good reason for this advice. If you use your bedroom for everything from working out to streaming *Stranger Things*, you're confusing your brain.

Don't ignore this advice when it comes to your work life.

If your workspace is at the kitchen counter or in the middle of the living room, you'll be constantly distracted. (Oh look, the washing machine's done! Time for another load.)

More importantly, you'll have a difficult time "punching out" at the end of your workday.

It's tough enough to separate work and personal life when you work for yourself, but even more so when you don't have at least some sort of physical boundary or don't move physically between the two spaces.

Granted, that ship has sailed — the lines between work and personal lives/spaces are blurred in this age of remote work. But the point is that without a designated workspace, you'll never feel like your workday has ended.

And wasn't that "always-on, always-connected" feeling one of the reasons you left the corporate world? You're not going to achieve any better work-life balance if you don't learn how to turn off the "Open" sign.

As a business owner, you feel like you're on the clock all the time. After all, some of your best ideas may come to you in the shower. A designated office space won't change that — but at least you remind yourself that you "left the building" and you have better things to do.

You don't need a lot of space for this to work.

My first home office was in a tiny walk-in closet that could fit nothing but my desk. I faced a wall and felt just a tad closed in; I had to roll out my chair if I wanted to close the door. But when office hours were over, you bet I "stepped out of the office" (literally) and closed that door.

These days, I'm lucky to have a spacious office on a different floor from our main living space. When I go upstairs after work, I have zero temptation to return to my computer downstairs unless I'm deliberately pulling off a 12-hour day to meet a deadline.

If you don't have a spare closet or bedroom, try to claim a corner somewhere, ideally in a room that gets the least traffic.

If you can, add a physical separator, like a folding room divider or a short bookcase, between your corner and the rest of the room. It's a simple but effective act to physically enter or leave the office space at the beginning and at the end of your workday.

The minute you enter, you have told yourself you're ready to go and focus on whatever you need to do to run and grow your business.

The minute you leave, you remind yourself that your business is not your entire life, and you give yourself permission to prioritize yourself and your family.

All that said, don't keep this rule so rigid that you're always glued to your desk.

Personally, I only work at my actual desk some of the time, which is a shame because I have a nice Mac Studio computer with a 27-inch screen. But I have a comfy couch in my office, and I prefer to work there on my laptop and only use the desk to work while standing.

I also roam around the house sometimes, working outside on my back patio or in the living room. But I'm not easily distracted.

Even when the fam is watching TV, I'm completely oblivious and unaware of what's happening around me because I'm in my own bubble. I might as well be on a different planet because, I kid you not, I wouldn't hear the doorbell or realize someone is running the vacuum cleaner right next to my feet.

(Read the little side story about the advantages and perils of my "I'm here physically but somewhere else mentally" technique. Or, if you're already a master at zoning out, feel free to meet me in Part II.)

Pro Tip

If you have a designated office, you don't need to go over-board decorating it, but make the environment comfort-able and productive.

Years ago, I read advice that your office shouldn't be too "homey" because it will take away from your business mode and make you less productive. Whatever.

My office has a comfy love seat, lots of plants, and original art. I'm comfortable and productive, thank you very much, even if some parts of my office look like a living room.

(My bookshelf and other businessy furniture don't show in my video meetings, so someone actually said to me once on a call that they thought it was my living room).

Other advice you may read recommends not facing a window because you would get distracted. I suppose you could, if you haven't mastered "the zone" habit (see "Zone Out" sidebar, next page).

My take is that you should find your own zen as long as your workspace is ergonomic and you enjoy it long enough to get your work done.

Did I mention that you can deduct your office space (and furnishings) for a little tax break, at least in the United States? Check the IRS literature about home office allow-ances and ask your CPA about business deductions for the furnishings.

Sidebar, Purely for the Entertainment Factor: Learning to Zone Out on Cue

< Scene 1, somewhere in rural Washington >

Two teenagers sit on the couch in the living room, blasting at each other on the TV screen with virtual weapons while talking to invisible friends via their PlayStation headsets. Their little brother is banging with cars nearby.

Next to the living room, in the kitchen, their grandmother puts away dishes, which clank as she skillfully distributes them. A big, black dog barks at her, begging for a treat.

In the doorless room that opens to the kitchen on one side and the living room on the other, a woman sits at a desk in the corner. She's oblivious to the domestic symphony all around her, typing furiously on a keyboard. It's as if she's in a parallel universe, or perhaps she's deaf.

< End of scene >

You guessed it, I'm that woman. And my hearing is perfectly fine. This was more than a decade ago, when we had three generations living under one roof in our old house. My office was in the line of fire of the kitchen on one side and the living room on the other — and no door on either side.

The office was architecturally challenged, meaning the odd angles of the wall and other complications put the door-making idea beyond my husband's DIY skills and beyond my budget for a professional job.

It all started when I had to give up my "real" office in a spare bedroom on the other side of the house so my parents could move in with us after emigrating from Europe. When we prepared for their arrival, I had to vacate my workspace. My only choice for relocation was the semi-enclosed dining room.

My husband did a beautiful job converting one of the three dining room entrances into a wall. But anything else would be pushing it.

An office without doors didn't seem like a problem at the time. After all, the two older boys were already trained to follow my "not available right now" cues.

For example, if they knocked on my old office door and didn't hear an answer, it meant I was on the phone and they had to wait quietly. A doorless arrangement was a matter of a little retraining, right?

That, of course, was before we had a new baby. Have you tried to cue in a newborn or a toddler that it was time to be quiet?

So, I adapted.

When I needed to make a quiet phone call while the rest of the domestics roamed around, I stepped into the bedroom. And to focus the rest of the time, I learned to ignore the world by creating a sound-proof bubble around me.

Think of a ghost movie scenario when everybody goes about their business without hearing or seeing the ghosts' antics — except the ghosts were the other people outside of my bubble.

Problem is, we, humans, have reflexes.

If someone came up to me and said something while I was in the bubble, I may have nodded my head without actually hearing what was being said, and if the person told me later that they came and talked to me, I denied any such fact. And I wasn't lying (at least from my point of view).

At other times, I sort of heard what the intruder was telling me, and I may have even answered, but I later had no recollection of this interaction.

So, we set a new rule. When I am in "the zone" — which is basically any time I'm on my computer — if I don't turn my head, stop typing, and acknowledge you, you're pretty much talking to the walls. It means I'm with you physically but not in spirit. Period.

My family learned to cope fairly well under these new regulations, but they did like to make fun of me occasionally. Sometimes, the teens would swear I turned/stopped/acknowledged when I didn't recall, for example, giving them permission to watch TV.

I was vindicated eventually with proof that I am not crazy while watching a TV episode of *Castle*.

Richard Castle is a bestselling fiction writer who moonlights as a sidekick to a police detective. His teenage daughter insisted one day that they discussed some issue that required parental input. When he couldn't recall it, he asked her something to the effect of, "Honey, was I typing?" (or maybe, "Sweetheart, was I in 'the zone?'" or maybe even, "Yes, but did I look *at* you or *through* you?").

Now we have it on good authority that "the zone" exists.

With a little practice, you, too, can find it. Just stay out of mine.

Spotlight on: Amanda Scheldt

Business name: Infinity Content
Location: Greater St. Lous area, Missouri
Founded: 2020
Business structure: LLC
Website: infinitycontentsolutions.com

Amanda Scheldt is a content writer and researcher for security-based companies. She worked in a variety of industries and pivoted to cybersecurity in 2017, earning a master's degree in the field and working for several prominent companies.

Amanda had an existing blog when she found herself unemployed and at a crossroads in 2020 after 17 years in the workforce. The blog allowed her to segue into freelance writing for extra money while job searching.

In 2021, she took an unconventional path and started a small Etsy writing shop for small businesses to book affordable writing services from her, which eventually led to her first three retainer clients.

Amanda's growth in the cybersecurity space has since increased exponentially, and she hopes to reach a point in the future where she has enough work to bring in a part-time support team.

What was your biggest challenge when you first got started?
Finding clients and selling my expertise. I still struggle with this one from time to time because I don't feel I am as good a writer as I should be.

How did you overcome it?
I started by throwing my hat into the ring with hot leads I found from freelancing and content marketing groups I belong to. It took

me a good three-plus months after I started doing this to actually land a few clients for myself.

What was your biggest mistake in terms of operations, and how did you fix it?

Not realizing the expense beyond running a business. My first full year of freelancing was challenging because I didn't understand what I truly needed for my business to run successfully. I got stuck in a shiny object syndrome situation and bought tools that hindered rather than benefited me.

So, I literally went back to using mostly spreadsheets for everything. I know it sounds so archaic but when you have limited/inconsistent income, you need to pay attention to the expense of things. Not just purchase and deploy a tool if it's going to make processes either the same or more time-consuming to use for your business successfully.

How has your business grown, and how did that growth come about?

My business has grown steadily year after year. I typically have between four and seven regular clients working with me. Some need consistent support and others are more ad hoc. A lot of that business growth has come from networking and building a solid referral network.

What has been the best part about the path you've chosen as a business owner?

The short answer is the freedom and flexibility of doing my own thing. Many people don't know this, but aside from being on unemployment when I started freelancing, I was also the primary caretaker for my grandmother until her passing in 2021. She was one of the only immediate family I had left in the area. So, this path afforded us a lot of time together weekly.

I also realize I have been blessed in that I once worked from home for a company during a time when that was essentially nonexistent for most people. However, I was still busy and felt "chained to my desk and office" daily.

Self-employment doesn't make me feel that way on most days. If I don't get my day going until after 10 a.m., why stress myself if I know I will still make the deadlines for my clients?

What's next for you?

My goals for the next year or two are to grow my network and build a stronger foundation in business. This path is not always about the money for me. I am confident enough in my skills and expertise to know that I will always be able to make money, so my goal is to focus on finding more balance.

I spent the past few years doing limited traveling and focusing on growing professionally. I plan to continue upskilling, too, to further grow my expertise and share it with my clients for their content needs.

PART II

Setting Up Your Freelance Business

Part II covers the four business components introduced in the previous chapter: infrastructure, processes, tools and systems, and roadmap.

I break down the components into three buckets:

Tier 1: Must-have before you get started or as soon as possible thereafter

Tier 2: Nice-to-have but not a high priority; something to consider once you've got some projects rolling

Tier 3: Highly recommended if you want to uplevel your game

These tiers offer a lot of flexibility, and you should base them on your own priorities and specific situation. I note here and there which processes or tools can fall into multiple tiers, depending on what's important to you.

And if you need a more linear, step-by-step "map" that includes all four components together broken down by tiers, grab a cheat sheet at freelancerscompass.com/cheatsheet.

Chapter 3

Infrastructure

(Loose) category definition: Anything that impacts the financial and legal aspects of your business

> *Often it isn't the mountains ahead that wear you out; it's the little pebble in your shoe."*
>
> *— Muhammad Ali*

Tier 1

Business structure

Whether you think of yourself as a business owner or a gig worker, once you earn money from freelancing, the IRS views your work as a business activity. That means you must choose a business structure, which will impact how that activity is taxed.

Typically, the decision comes down to three choices: solo, limited liability corporation (LLC), and S-corporation. Some of the rules are a bit complicated, particularly when it comes to LLCs, but in a nutshell:

- **Solo:** You and your business are one entity. Your business income is included on your personal federal tax return on Schedule C; you also pay self-employment tax on your net profit. To pay yourself, you simply take an "owner draw" out of the business funds.

- **Limited liability corporation:** Unless you have a business partnership, you're a single-member LLC, which means the IRS simply disregards your LLC status. You report business income via Schedule C, same as you would as a solo operator. The rules are more complicated if you have multiple LLC members.

- **S-corporation:** Your business is its own entity. You must pay yourself as an employee, collect income and Social Security taxes every payroll cycle, and remit your employee and your corporate portions to the IRS. Any profit after expenses (which include payroll) are considered dividends rather than a draw. These dividends are taxed the same as any other personal income, so you don't pay self-employment tax.

Many, if not most, freelancers start out as solopreneurs (it's cheaper and simpler), but some decide later to change their structure either for legal or financial reasons.

I was a solo business for the first two decades and didn't see the need to incorporate until I got close to six figures. That's when I finally paid a CPA for a consult, and he advised me I should have switched when I hit $60K a year, which would have saved me a couple of thousand dollars or more in federal income taxes.

Pro Tip

Do think about your business structure early on.

Rules may vary in your state, but in my state, Washington, you can't keep the same business name when you go from solo to a corporation (but you can if moving from LLC to S-corp and vice versa).

When I incorporated, I had to change my company name, get a new business license, open a new bank account, redo any automatic payments coming from my bank account, complete new W9s with all current customers, and switch my payment info with every single accounts payables department.

If you want to avoid this hassle, pay a CPA for a half-hour or one-hour consult before you choose your structure; the investment is well worth it. You can find lots of free resources online, as well as free advice in person (see Chapter 8 for info on SCORE), but the value of these freebies is limited because it's not custom-tailored to your situation.

Business license (and name)

Okay, a business license may be more of a Tier 1-ish. You could argue it's Tier 2, and you wouldn't be wrong. You don't need it to get clients or to pay your taxes (except: see the next section, "Business bank account"). Plus, in some jurisdictions, you don't need one if you're a solo operator and haven't met a certain revenue threshold.

But really, why postpone it?

You'll need one sooner or later, so you might as well commit to it now.

It will cost you little, and it instantly elevates you from amateur status to pro when you legitimize your enterprise. On some (admittedly rare) occasions, a license may even be one of the criteria that a potential client will use to vet you.

Check to see if your city or county requires a license as well. Often, the state license is a one-time deal, but the local jurisdiction requires annual renewal.

You may be able to fly under the radar of your local entity for a while. But eventually, they'll get wind of your new business (in fact, the state licensing office may be sharing the info automatically). Why take the risk of a retroactive penalty?

Lastly, check with your local taxing entities on any other requirements, as they may have some additional, seemingly random fees.

(One county I lived in required home-based businesses to get a cottage business license. It cost 10 times more than the state business license, and the county didn't enforce it unless a neighbor made a complaint about noise or nuisance. You can guess how high the compliance rate was for "invisible," quiet businesses. Let's just say it wasn't Tier 1 or 2 for me. If I hadn't moved to another county years later, I would have filed the paperwork someday. Probably.)

Before you file for a license, you get to agonize over your biggest business decision: choosing a name. Just kidding.

Don't overthink it. Really.

You can name your business anything you want as long as someone else hasn't claimed it. You can always add a DBA (doing business as) later for a punchier, public-facing, marketing-friendly name.

You may want to check the URL availability before you choose a name.

My solo business name was Tollefson Creative Solutions. Which is ironic because I was as creative as vanilla ice cream when I chose it. I marketed myself under my own name (you're your own brand and all that), and my clients didn't give a hoot.

When I had to choose a new name to incorporate, I spent hours putting different spins on Latin words, creating word mash-ups, and using all sorts of other tricks to come up with something clever. I had an entire business retreat (more on this later in Chapter 5) devoted to it. I even posted a poll for my friends to vote on their favorite.

The winner, nMeta Communications, Inc., was perfect.

One, because meta means "outside of normal limits of something" and "seeing something from a higher perspective instead of from within," which describes how I like to think. Two, nMeta stands for engaging, meaningful, and targeted — which is how I describe the content I deliver.

And then, six months later, this little company called Facebook decided to rebrand itself as Meta.

Guess who has two new DBAs (Audacia Tech Content and Audacia MarCom) on the business license now? Yep, not Meta.

There's no way I'm changing my legal company name again, so all the paperwork continues to live under nMeta Communications. And my clients still couldn't care less.

My DBAs are really an overkill, if I'm honest. After incorporation, I continued to market myself under my own name (my website URL remains seattletechnologywriter.com).

But I dabbled with the idea of creating an agency, and marketing it under nMeta would have been iffy. I don't want any confusion about a potential association with Meta, nor do my services have anything to do with the metaverse — except, of course, if a client wants me to write content for or about it.

Moral of the story: You can agonize about a business name and be pleased as punch when you come up with something creative and unique, only to have the rug pulled from under your feet thanks to an ambitious, if not misguided, CEO's pet project.

So don't waste too much energy on it; your time is better spent on other marketing activities that bring in clients and cash flow.

Business bank account

If you're operating a solo business under your own name, you technically don't need a separate account for your business. But if you're still with me, you understand by now that there's a difference between doing the minimum required and following best practices.

A separate account for your business keeps things nice and tidy for accounting. You can easily keep track of cash flow and pay for your business expenses without commingling business and personal funds.

If your business ever gets audited by your state or another business tax authority, you're not giving the auditors any reasons to poke around your personal finances.

Keep in mind that if you use a business name, you will need your business license first — your bank will request it when you open the new account.

As a solo practitioner, you may not need a business account per se — some banks will simply add your business name as a DBA to a consumer account so you can cash checks written to your business. Regardless, this account should be separate from your personal one.

Pro Tip

One way larger companies vet their vendors (you!) is by looking up their Dun & Bradstreet profile. D&B is a business intel and analytics company that a variety of organizations use for purposes such as risk analysis and research.

You can get a D-U-N-S number from D&B for free and create a profile for your company. Feed some basic data into the profile and D&B populates it further with info from its own sources.

Here's a little story to incentivize you to set up the right structure early on.

I had a solid profile for my solo company, showing it was in business for 20-some years, etc. Since I had to rename the company when I incorporated, I had to start at square one with my D-U-N-S number.

I almost cried when I learned that D&B would not carry over my business longevity and track record into the new corp, even though I tried to explain to them it's the exact same business with the same types of services and simply a new business structure.

My new company is an infant as far as D&B and the people who use its database are concerned. Not a big deal except that at a cursory glance, it looks like I've been in business for less than five years and am still a startup (which a client who doesn't know my track record may consider a higher risk).

Just my luck, the first time I was asked for my D-U-N-S was right after I had to create this new profile, when a very large company engaged me directly. Fortunately, the paperwork was a procurement formality because my client already chose me. But I'm still salty about D&B.

Tier 2

Lawyer-reviewed contracts

First: Never, ever do any work without a written agreement.

Note that I included the descriptor "lawyer-reviewed." That's because written agreements by themselves, whether you call them contracts or something else, are a Tier 1 must-have; whereas a lawyer's input is in the Tier 2 nice-to-have bucket.

It doesn't matter if your client is a friend, a family member, a harmless tween neighbor, or the Dalai Lama.

You must agree on the price, terms, and conditions. Upfront. In a documented fashion. Which could literally be one or two paragraphs.

Some people may tell you that an agreement could be as simple as an email that's been acknowledged by both parties. I'm not disagreeing, but I'm not qualified to advise you on this. Best to ask a legal professional.

In any case, a written agreement is the only way to manage scope creep, avoid surprises or misunderstandings on either end, set expectations, and more.

As I mentioned, an agreement doesn't have to be ten pages of legalese. (Although I promise you, that's what you'll get, typically, if you work with some very large enterprises or some very paranoid startups.)

Second, never, ever sign a contract without reading it closely and making sure you understand what you're agreeing to.

It's tempting, especially when you really need the work, to sign a contract after skimming it or ignoring everything that might as well be written in Chinese (which is likely 90% of the document). But you may be shocked to learn the outrageous terms some companies include.

One startup that wanted to hire me had a 12-page contract filled with overreaching terms that mentioned my spouse and estate in one clause, and included a statement that said, "This agreement shall be deemed as having been prepared jointly by both parties." Jointly my keister. Hard pass.

When you're starting out, you likely don't have the capital to invest in a lawyer. In that case, you must educate yourself as much as you can so you understand as much as possible what to include in a contract (if you're writing one yourself) or what you're agreeing to (if your client company requires its own, in-house contract, which you may not be able to negotiate).

You'll find plenty of info online about the much-loathed indemnity clauses and a few others that most independent contractors would trade for a root canal. Anesthesia-free. Find resources that will translate all that lawyer-speak into plain English (see Chapter 8 for some ideas).

Many (most?) client-provided contracts, possibly written by an entire legal team, are one-sided and not in your favor. If your client has a standard contract, you can bank on the terms providing all the protections and then some for the client — and zero for you.

You can ask for modifications, additions, or (gasp!) deletions. Some companies will allow minor changes, especially on smaller things, if you make the business case for them.

Others will allow you to add some of your own additional terms to their template. But they're less likely to budge on big stuff like work for hire, indemnification, and similar clauses. In my experience, those are more likely a take-it-or-leave-it situation. If you're lucky, you may be able to narrow some of the very broad terms.

Try negotiating, nonetheless, and know your deal-breakers.

I want to say you're not losing anything by negotiating, but I'd be lying. I had two would-be clients ghost me after I brought up a few questions to clarify the contract or pointed out areas I'd like modified or couldn't agree to. It's a small risk and truly an anomaly. To me, the bigger risk is having unnecessary terms that I may regret later.

Side note: Do check your state's laws, as some of the standard contract terms may be illegal in your location. For example, Washington doesn't allow noncompete clauses for independent contractors, regardless of where the client is based.

Not that you should agree to noncompetes even if they're legal. Your client has many privileges, but telling you whom you can do business with is not one of them.

A noncompete clause severely impacts your ability to produce income. If a client wants exclusivity, they better be willing to reward you handsomely for it (in real dollars, not "visibility" or other such nonsense).

Once in a while, when all the planets are aligned or the sun has eclipsed, you will get that one client-written contract that doesn't have any disagreeable terms and is impressively freelancer-friendly.

After you confirm that it's not a dream and you're not in the Matrix, you'll dance like no one's watching and frame the contract on your wall.

Fine, maybe you won't dance. You'll at least be amazed, if not rejoice, at your good fortune, knowing that it's not likely to happen again any time soon.

All this to say: As soon as you can afford a little "splurge," hire a lawyer to review your most important contracts, at least the clauses you can't understand or are the most critical.

It's not cheap, and the chances of a legal issue arising in work like marketing content or strategy are very small. But, like anything that provides you protection (and peace of mind), this is money well spent.

The same applies to your own contracts. You can get away with using online templates and even cobbling together a contract by copying clauses you like out of various other clients' contracts. I did that, too, before I had a lawyer.

At some point, it's worth having your own attorney check out your vendor contract template to make sure it's customized to your exact situation. It will set you back a few hundred dollars, but it's a one-time, fully deductible investment that helps you minimize your business risk.

Pro Tip

Check all your local business tax codes as part of your due diligence. You may discover all sorts of fun things you'll have to pay for as a privilege of doing business.

Some examples:

Business and occupation tax or similar

In Washington state, businesses pay revenue tax based on gross income, with very few deductions, even if they don't make any profit. Those that earn under a specified amount can file for exempt status, and I blissfully enjoyed that exemption for the first few years in business.

Inventory tax

One county where I lived taxed businesses on their inventory and business property like computer equipment (I was flabbergasted!). Luckily, someone could apply for an exemption if their business property value was under a certain threshold. (Yay! More savings for me).

Sales tax

Most states have a sales tax, but don't levy it on the same type of products and services equally. For instance, some impose tax on consulting or professional services (which writing and marketing typically fall under) and on digital products (like downloadable assets), while others don't. Some base the sales tax on where the sale originates, while others on the destination. And so forth. Talk about an accounting nightmare!

Tier 3

Lawyer-reviewed contracts for your service providers

Same drill as before: Don't hire any contractors or other professional service providers without a contract.

It's the same song and dance as with your own clients: You may want to provide your own contract, or the vendors may bring their own. The bottom line is: Don't outsource without a written agreement.

You can create your own contract without legal help, but at some point, you may want your attorney to review it and make sure you're not missing anything important.

It's especially a good idea to consult a lawyer if you plan to hire foreign contractors. Different countries have their own laws about independent workers and business contracts, and you may need to conform to those rules.

(If your contractor is considered an employee according to local law, you may be required to establish a legal business entity locally. One solution to explore as a workaround is an "employer of record," or EOR, service. An EOR is a third party that hires the local employees and manages payroll and other employment on your behalf, keeping you compliant with the law.)

If you're good with your vendor providing their own contract or they insist on it (as is often the case with VAs), make sure you add any of your own terms that you consider nonnegotiable to that contract.

Additionally, consider asking your subcontractors to sign a separate nondisclosure agreement (NDA) so they have clarity on what information is confidential and how you expect them to treat that information.

Pro Tip

It's common for clients to have a master service agreement (MSA) that covers the general terms but doesn't list particulars such as scope and fee. In this case, a separate statement of work (SoW) document typically spells out the details for each individual project.

If your client has both an MSA and SoWs, try to include some of your standard terms in the SoW that you couldn't add to the master contract. This strategy also works well if you forgo contracts altogether in favor of SoWs (if the client is agreeable to it).

I prefer only SoWs in most cases (with my attorney's blessing), and I include a few clauses in the SoW from my contract template, such as limitation of liability.

Common contract clauses
Specific contract language is beyond the scope of this book, but briefly, a few terms or clauses that are common in contracts include:

• Description of services and deliverables
• Duration of contract and termination terms
• Fees,* invoicing, and payment terms
• Confidentiality
• Work product or intellectual property ownership (for example, unlike articles published by the more traditional media outlets, marketing content is more likely to be "work for hire")
• Indemnification
• Liability
• Warranty
• Independent contractor relationship

*See Chapter 8 for a few websites where you can learn more.

Business insurance

Business insurance comes in a variety of flavors, including general liability, professional liability (including error and omissions), and business continuity.

As an independent contractor, general liability and professional liability are the most likely types of policies you may want to consider.

General liability applies more to those instances when you have customers coming to your premises. These policies may have other protections, such as damage to or loss of your equipment and possibly damage from fire or earthquake.

These are areas you may be able to cover under your homeowners' insurance. So if you decide you want this protection, start there first.

Professional liability is the more important piece, in my view. It covers you for things like negligence and defamation claims.

Not all policies are the same, so make sure you understand your coverage. For example, copyright infringement may not be covered under an errors and omissions (E&O) policy but may be covered under a media liability policy, which is a subset of E&O.

Ask lots of questions before you sign up, and read your policy carefully. You'll likely find that insurance policies are also written by lawyers who don't speak normal people's English, but you can call your insurer and ask for an interpretation.

Each of these policies shouldn't set you back more than about $500–$1,500 a year. Several companies (biBerk and Hiscox, among others) have a very easy purchasing process online.

You could also speak with a local insurance broker to see if you can save a little money.

When I bought my first general liability policy, I saw a broker in person (remember those days?). She asked me a few detailed questions about the type of work I do to make sure I wasn't paying for coverage I didn't need. I don't know if I saved any money, but I certainly didn't pay more. And it was reassuring to walk through my case — live! — with a professional.

Some clients will require you to carry general liability or professional liability, both, or possibly more. Push to get out of any requirements that don't apply to you.

For example, you shouldn't need commercial auto insurance if you're not going to drive for your client's engagement. Alternatively, your personal auto insurance may allow you to add your client as a named party. Another example is unemployment or workers' compensation insurance. You don't need it if you don't have any employees other than yourself.

I can't emphasize this enough: Only use my advice as a starting point. When it comes to risk, it's best to discuss your needs with a professional before you decide your course of action. For example, it will cost you nothing to speak with a qualified insurance professional, yet it may help you avoid mistakes.

Recap

Your Quick To-Do Checklist for Setting Up Infrastructure

Now:

- ✓ Business structure
- ✓ Business name
- ✓ Business license
- ✓ Business bank account

Now or later:

- ✓ Contract templates
- ✓ Business insurance

Get your step-by-step cheat sheet with all four components together broken down by tiers at freelancerscompass.com/cheatsheet, where you can also schedule a complimentary, 20-minute coaching session with me.

Spotlight on: Diane Faulkner

Business name: Full Circle Press
Location: Jacksonville, Florida
Founded: May 1999
Business structure: Sole proprietor
Website: fullcirclepress.net

Diane Faulkner is a writer, editor, ghostwriter, speaker, and content marketing strategist who's been a solopreneur for 25 years. While her main niche is employment law, she also writes frequently about finance, technology, and health.

Diane had a corporate career for 17 years, primarily in human resources. She freelanced on the side for journals and magazines for a while before realizing she could make a good living working for herself doing what she enjoyed.

After filing for her business license in 1999, Diane never looked back. Within a year of becoming serious about her writing, she matched her corporate salary. Diane started ghostwriting leadership books for international CEOs, and as the internet took off, she began writing articles for major companies like LegalZoom, U.S. News and World Report, and Forbes.

What compelled you to start freelancing?

I had reached the top of where I was going professionally. I enjoyed being a mentor to others in my corporate position, and I found that by writing, I reached a larger audience. Doors opened for me. I started speaking and appearing on radio, television, podcasts, and vid-casts (I don't know the word for that at the moment).

What was your biggest challenge when you first got started, and how did you overcome it?

Figuring out how to get more clients. I went to a writers conference and learned how to market myself. I'd never heard about writers conferences until an artist friend of mine told me about this one.

What was the biggest surprise about going from a corporate career to running a business?

How freeing it is to be in business for myself. Yes, there are tedious things that have to be done, but scheduling is everything. If I need or want time off, I schedule it.

What was your biggest mistake in terms of operations, and how did you fix it?

In the beginning, my biggest mistake was not scheduling out different operational duties for myself. I'd go from writing to accounting to marketing willy-nilly, and it kind of burned me out until I found or created tools to help me stay on schedule. I created tools, like checklists (as opposed to to-do lists), and found tools, like CRMs and timeclocks, to help me keep on track.

How has your business grown, and how did that growth come about?

My business has grown from simply writing feature articles for trades to writing books, scripts, playbooks, e-books, whitepapers, speaking, you name it. Actively seeking out writer communities, learning from others, and mostly having accountability partners has propelled my growth.

Have you ever thought about going back to corporate employment and why? If yes, what happened?

I've had my low points where I thought about going back to corporate. Downturns in the economy that affect marketing budgets can put a damper on my ability to get clients. I went so far as to interview with a company once; I turned down the job. I just couldn't let go of my freedom, and I had faith I would overcome.

What's your one piece of advice to someone making or contemplating the switch?

Get involved in professional organizations or groups and pick people's brains. Listen to their stories. Learn what's involved in marketing yourself.

What's next for you?

Writing books under my own byline.

Chapter 4

Processes

Loose category definition: Anything describing how you typically do business, both for client-facing and backend (internal) activities.

> *And those who were seen dancing were thought to be crazy by those who could not hear the music."*
>
> — *Friedrich Nietzsche*

TIER 1

Payment and invoicing

Before you negotiate your first contract or SoW, decide on your payment terms.

If you let clients lead this decision, you may be stuck with something like invoicing at the end of the month with terms net 30 (payment within 30 calendar days). Imagine that you complete a project during the first week of the month and then have to wait for almost two months to get paid. Not a great way to manage cash flow.

Just because your client's standard terms are 30 days doesn't mean you have to go along with that.

My terms are net 15, while writers I know have net 7 or even payable on receipt. Many clients will honor your terms, but you have to be clear about them before you accept the project.

The smaller the company, the more likely it will oblige. Large enterprises are the worst, including various tech giants — they pay vendors in 60 or 90 days after invoicing and will absolutely not deviate. (Don't you just feel their love for small businesses?).

As a small vendor, you likely won't be working with very large corporations directly, at least not frequently. You're more likely to get work from big brands through marketing agencies, and agencies are more flexible. Some will still stick to their guns, which may be net 30, but others will allow you to set your own terms or at least meet you halfway.

If the terms the client is willing to offer you are simply not palatable, see if you can find a workaround. You may not succeed, but it's worth a try.

I had a large client whose nonnegotiable payment terms were 45 days after invoicing. I was not enthused to jump on that train, especially since it was a monthly retainer and an annual contract. I explained to the project manager that I wouldn't be interested if we couldn't agree on more favorable terms, particularly since a retainer arrangement guaranteed my availability.

I asked if I could invoice in advance — on the first of the month — for the following month's deliverable. That would mean I would be paid mid month for the current month's fee. The company's procurement department allowed prebilling, and I worked those terms into the SoW. Score for the little guy!

A deposit is another standard component of payment terms for professional services.

For marketing work, for example, 50% is fairly standard. Some writers and strategists deviate a bit; for example, invoicing 50% after kickoff or a 30/30/40 split (30% upfront, 30% with first draft, 40% upon completion, or similar milestones).

My standard is a 50% deposit prior to kickoff. For returning clients with a good payment track record, I'll invoice for the deposit as soon as we sign the SoW, but won't wait for the money before launching. I'll also switch to the 30/30/40 format for projects that have multiple deliverables or a very high package price.

When you're a newly independent contractor, you may be uncomfortable asking for a deposit or talking about money in general. I feel you. I was there for more than 10 years.

I didn't ask for deposits regularly, charged way too low, and didn't raise my rates for years. I simply hated negotiating with clients.

Guess when I started earning a much better living? Yep, when I had my duh! moment and came out of my ignorant (timid?) phase — with a little help from coaches.

That's when I overhauled my fees, started regularly increasing those fees as demand grew, and made the deposit nonnegotiable in most cases. A common exception is agencies, which I'm okay with because they bring projects from big names and I don't have to wait 60–90 days for payment while also getting great portfolio pieces.

Research the standard practices. Talk to your peers and seasoned freelancers. Seek out mentors. Attend professional development workshops discussing client-negotiation topics. Work with a coach if you can splurge on it at this stage.

Use all this intel to figure out what works best for you and what areas you're willing to keep flexible, then approach the client discussion with a professional detachment. (Money discussions are never personal!)

Sure, some may flinch at your rates or the request for a deposit. Don't second-guess yourself about it. Their reaction may be more about their own inexperience working with contractors or about a budget that's not aligned with market rates.

Know your value and how to explain it (and how it translates into your fees), and don't hesitate to walk away from a project that's completely out in left field.

It's scary to lose an income opportunity. But devaluing your service doesn't keep you in business, either. At least not in a thriving way.

Certainly, do what you have to do to pay bills while you're still building momentum. But keep working at increasing your value, explaining it better, and finding higher-quality clients who see that value and will pay for it — and you won't be staying in this survival mode for much longer.

A word about invoicing: The invoice itself doesn't need to be fancy.

It can be as simple as an Excel or Word template (that's what I used when I first got started). The idea is to spend a few minutes creating one, so all you have to do is quickly fill in some fields and send it off.

As you move into Tier 2, you'll want something a little more sophisticated, like an accounting app that will not only create invoices for you but also track past-due payments, income and expenses, and the overall financial health of your business. (See Chapter 5 for more tools.)

Pro Tip

If the idea of discussing money gives you the heebie-jee-bies, know that savvy clients are used to negotiating, unless it's their first rodeo, too. It's how the business world goes round.

Remember that price is not the only thing you can negotiate. You can also negotiate deadlines, scope, number of revision rounds, and various other areas that make the project more compelling besides income.

As my marketing coach Ilise Benun recommends, ask for what you want. You may be surprised that you'll receive it more often than not.

A few years ago, I interviewed Amy Hardison White — an Austin, Texas, freelance writer and content strategist for software-as-a-service companies — for an article, and I'll never forget her advice.

"If you don't negotiate, you're setting yourself up for possibly getting pushed back in the future," she said. "I always try to push myself to ask for X percent more — for what makes me uncomfortable but not want to jump out of my skin."

I'm still learning how to do this!

Even after 25 years in business, I'm constantly evaluating and adjusting my mindset.

The process of your personal and professional growth and business development never stops.

Expense tracking

This one goes without saying, but if you're not used to it, tracking expenses for your business takes a little habit-building. You need receipts for anything you want to deduct — and you may be surprised by the various expenses that are considered deductible.

Best to check with your CPA, but my CPA's long list of suggested business deductions included some things I would never think of myself, like eyeglasses (I need them to do my work!) and a watch (needed to get to client meetings on time).

Anything from professional development and business workshops to work-related books and internet access is fair game.

Again, please don't take my word for it — get professional advice. The IRS also has some publications for small businesses, but those are almost as much fun to read as contracts.

The most important thing to know about expense tracking is that you need all your receipts (in case you get audited) and a tracking system. The latter can be as simple as a spreadsheet, but as your business (and overhead) grows, you may want a tool built specifically for small business accounting.

There are tons of options for reasonably priced, cloud-based apps — such as FreshBooks, Zoho, and Wave — that small operations commonly use.

Personally, I've used the desktop version of QuickBooks for more than a decade and could not push myself toward the cloud-based version (for various reasons, the main one being loss of control of where my data lives). Recently, I finally had to bite the bullet because Intuit (the company that owns QuickBooks) forced my hand by sunsetting its desktop app.

If you're planning to pay yourself through payroll, you may want to ensure your bookkeeping app integrates with the payroll service. That will save you the pain on manually entering your paycheck data into your books, so you can reconcile your account.

Pro Tip

At some point in your solopreneur journey, you may want to talk with a financial planner.

Someday, you may want to retire. You'll need to stash away some money in advance, which is not easy to do when you don't have HR breathing down your neck to complete your 401K enrollment.

The great news is that you have several options for retirement planning as a solopreneur, but you'll most definitely want an expert to guide you through them.

Of course, many of us may never truly retire in the traditional sense of the word. And that's by choice — we blaze our own trail even in "retirement."

But, even if you think you'll stay busy forever doing what makes you happy (ideally not working on client projects but on your own), you'll need to prepare financially.

TIER 2

Documented project delivery workflows

If you're delivering the same type of projects as you did in your old job, you already have an established workflow that you can adapt for clients.

You may have it committed to memory, but once you're past the stage of basic setup for your business, it's time to document your process, including steps and standard turnaround timelines.

Some common milestones for project workflows (once you've onboarded the client) and questions to answer include:

- **Kickoff:** How soon after signing the SoW or receiving the deposit do you typically schedule your client kickoff meeting? What is the typical agenda or the questions you want answered?

- **Discovery:** How long is your discovery window for different types of projects? What do you expect from the client during this time frame, and what should the client expect from you? How do you coordinate subject matter experts' interviews, if applicable?

- **Draft delivery:** What is your turnaround for the first round and revisions? How many rounds do you offer as part of your fee? How do you deliver the copy? How do you expect the client to provide feedback?

Some of these aspects may vary if you're allowing for flexibility to accommodate the client's internal process, but you should document your standard procedures nonetheless. And make sure to cover this during the kickoff so you and the client are on the same page.

Additionally, provide a schedule for each milestone, both your deadlines and the client's.

I have a Word template where I plug in every step, starting with the kickoff and delivery of supporting materials from the client and through the final delivery. I have standard turnarounds for each phase, depending on the project type. However, I ask clients before sending the schedule if those timelines provide them with adequate time, and I adjust dates as needed.

Documented workflows serve these three purposes, among others:

- You need to set and manage client expectations throughout your relationship. Your written SOPs ensure you're not forgetting any important pieces. No matter how many times you do this, you're bound to forget something because you're juggling dozens of balls.

- You're saving time because you don't have to think about it each time, and you can simply plug some dates into templates.

- You have a quick reference when a client asks you questions during your early conversations or when you need to add some timelines to your proposals.

In my proposal, I include typical milestones and turnarounds for drafts and client feedback, along with a high-level overview of how I approach projects. I also list the client's responsibilities so the prospect knows my process even before engaging me. If the proposal is accepted, I copy those sections into the SoW, which saves me time.

Onboarding and offboarding checklists

It took me a while to realize how much brainpower I could save with this, but I finally got a simple checklist (along with a folder with templates and documented SOPs) for my client onboarding.

The process is not that complicated — contract, SoW, 1099, deposit invoice, client intake form, etc. — but just the one-page checklist saves me from having to remember everything or moving prematurely to launch before all the prerequisite steps are completed.

My offboarding process, sadly, is my weak spot, and I'm pushing myself to button it up. My goal is to consistently request feedback from new clients at the end of the engagement — and, if I exceed expectations or receive a nice compliment, seize the opportunity to ask for referrals and a testimonial.

As much as I strive to deliver excellence every time, like any human, I sometimes miss the mark. Asking clients for feedback about performance is not only an opportunity to improve but also build stronger relationships and bring repeat business.

Computer security and backups

For me personally, this would be a Tier 1 item.

I'm including it here because you'll have a lot of other ducks to worry about when you're ramping up quickly. This is a basic list, so please treat it as a starting point.

File and computer backups

I don't have to tell you why you need backups, but since you probably didn't have to figure it out yourself in your old job, below are some very quick basics (speaking with my cybersecurity writer hat on).

Skip ahead if you already know the drill from your previous "employee awareness training," etc. at your former job.

Best practice is to follow the 3/2/1 backup method:

- At least three copies of your data (the original and two backups).

- Stored in two different mediums (for example, hard-drive partition, external drive, cloud).

- With at least one copy offsite (this could be the cloud, an offsite server, or a hard disk stored securely somewhere other than the building where your office is located).

When storing in the cloud, make sure the data is encrypted at rest and in transit (or end-to-end). Many consumer-grade file-storage apps don't have the strongest security, though they're getting better all the time. (I only recently learned that Dropbox is now finally encrypting data; what do you know!)

In addition to simply backing up your files, I strongly recommend you back up your entire hard drive, system and all.

On Macs, a simple way to do this is with the Time Machine (Windows may have something similar), but many cloud-backup apps also allow you to back up the entire system — which you can't do with file-storage apps like Dropbox, Box, etc.

Security tips

Security is a very broad topic and a complicated one to navigate, but you'll need to figure out eventually how to protect your company's data, especially if you handle confidential client information.

An antivirus/antimalware program and your computer's default firewall are a good start. However, they won't really protect you from all the types of threats and clever cybercriminals' shenanigans (or "tactics" if you love jargon).

Why would the cyber miscreants want your data when your solo business is such small potatoes?

I'm glad you asked.

They may not be targeting you directly, but they are targeting consumers with their consumer-grade security (or more likely, lack of) to steal data en masse.

If you're a slightly bigger potato, they may actually be targeting you to get to your customers (because small vendors are often the weak link in a bigger company's supply chain).

The point is, as you start making a little more money (if not before), you'll want to start thinking about some defenses that go beyond antivirus. And don't be surprised if your clients have a clause in your contract requiring you to follow cybersecurity practices to protect their data.

I'll cover a few security tools in Chapter 5, but here, let's talk about basic security processes, often referred to as cyber hygiene.

I'm going to refrain from going into full "cybersecurity-white-paper-writer mode" and spare you statistics and examples. Plus, as a savvy digital consumer, you likely already have good cybersecurity habits. But they are worth reiterating.

Again, skip ahead if you're already up to date on all this from your corporate life.

The following are just for starters and are not a comprehensive list by any stretch.

Keep your software up to date.

An incredible number of high-profile data breaches and major security incidents could have been avoided if only software and systems were patched with the latest security updates.

This is a big problem at large companies because they have such a massive footprint, but you have no excuse. The bad guys are automatically scanning for vulnerabilities to exploit, and you don't want to be swept up by that wave.

Use complicated, unique passwords (ideally as long as the website/app allows them).

Don't be one of the millions of unimaginative (or lazy) people whose password is 123456 or pa$$word. You're making it way too easy for someone to crack your accounts.

Think you're clever because you have a more complicated password that you're using for all accounts? Nope. Once one of the cloud apps or websites is breached, cybercriminals have got your number, or rather username and password.

Never store passwords in browsers, no matter how much they swear up and down about security.

And no, I don't expect you to have a photographic memory and remember 300 passwords that look like 59Jcoq9B!e5?nA66EQ4 (this is a very strong password, by the way) — read about password managers in Chapter 5.

Whatever you do, never, ever use your childhood nickname, child's birthday, name of your first crush, or other sentimental and memorable information for your password. Bad actors can find these juicy bits by combing social media and through all sorts of conniving means.

For that matter, forget pop culture names, events, trends, etc. Because anyone not living under a rock can guess them easily.

(Guess what were some of the most popular words used in passwords in recent years, depending on the season and a person's inclinations: covid, trump, and ukraine for those leaning into current affairs; freebritney, swiftie, bennifer, and loki for pop culture enthusiasts; george — as in, the adorable, tiny British prince — for fans of royalty.)

Use multifactor authentication (MFA) whenever you can.

It's not foolproof by far (and cybercriminals are learning how to break it more and more), but it does create one more hurdle for someone trying to access your accounts. (See Chapter 5 for recommended MFA authenticator apps.)

Learn to recognize signs of phishing, smishing (phishing via text), and vishing (phishing via phone).

These are all common ways for someone to steal your passwords and sensitive information.

And you can no longer rely on red flags like bad grammar that were a dead giveaway in the past. Cybercriminals have gotten quite skilled at creating authentic-looking phishing emails, and generative artificial intelligence is only making it easier for someone to craft a perfect message.

Use encryption for any files that are sensitive, confidential, etc.

Today's technology makes encrypting data much easier. For example, on a Mac, all you have to do is turn on your FileVault to encrypt your entire hard drive.

Keep in mind that email is not encrypted by default unless you use an email provider like Proton or PreVeil, so avoid sending sensitive data via email.

Don't use unsecured Wi-Fi (Wi-Fi that doesn't require a password).

Along the same lines, don't connect to random networks that you don't recognize, and be wary of public Wi-Fi even if it requires a password (e.g., at a hotel, coffee shop, etc.). Any data transmitted over these networks can be intercepted. Use your mobile phone as a hotspot or a virtual private network (VPN) (read about VPNs in Chapter 5).

Tier 3

Marketing SOPs

Although this isn't a book about marketing your business, marketing SOPs will help you streamline operations, hence I'm offering a few recommendations.

To be clear, marketing is something that you should be doing from the moment you decide to go solo.

As you work with more clients and establish a good process for prospecting, onboarding clients, and so on, you'll want to document your workflows and create templates eventually.

And if you decide to outsource some of your marketing activities to a VA, SOPs are a must. You can even make the SOP documentation your VA's first project. (I did.)

To create your SOPs, think through your outbound and inbound processes and how you move your prospect down your sales funnel all the way to signing the contract.

For outbound, you'll want to cover details like your channels (email, LinkedIn, etc.), how you qualify the leads, how frequently you do your outreach, and how soon you follow up.

Create a few email/LinkedIn/etc. templates for each scenario that can be customized for different situations.

Do the same for inbound inquiries, creating a workflow and templates for different scenarios that help you qualify your prospect, share portfolio and other information, set up a discovery call, send a proposal, etc. If you use a customer resource management (CRM) tool, you can set it up to align with your funnel so you can see all your prospects and their different phases in one location.

Emergency business SOPs

As a solopreneur, you don't have a team you can inform about an illness or another emergency that prevents you from following through on your commitments or who can notify clients if you can't make a meeting.

Life happens. As the saying goes, you could get hit by a bus tomorrow. Or a global pandemic could put you out of commission for a while.

In the event a major, unexpected event leaves you unable to communicate with clients for several days, it's a good idea to have an emergency plan that your VA, family member, or trusted friend can enact for you.

For my emergency SOPs, I have templates for emails to send to clients and contractors in the event I'm incapacitated for a while.

If I'm permanently unable to carry out business activities (e.g., I've been hit by a bus) and the business must be shut down, the emergency procedures kick into the next gear, with many others to be contacted (former clients, service providers, bookkeeper, and CPA) and additional steps to be taken to close out business accounts.

The SOPs describe the procedures for different types of emergencies and include templates for different situations and recipients. I also have an Excel spreadsheet with tabs for different categories of contacts. I do my best to keep my client roster on that list current, though I don't always succeed if I'm in between VAs.

Of course, in the event of my demise, none of these things will really be my problem. So, the business shutdown SOPs are for the benefit of my clients, as well as my family, whose job will be to wade through my affairs to wrap things up.

Pro Tip

Designate a main emergency contact for your emergency plan. This is the person who sets the wheels in motion. Then figure out who will be the executor of your emergency plan — this may not necessarily be the same person as the emergency contact.

Discuss with them ahead of time the plan and their roles. Make sure they know what's involved and where all the pertinent documents are located.

If your emergency is minor — say, you've been laid up with a virus for a few days or are having an emergency procedure that's not life-threatening — you could rely on a spouse or another close family member to be the executor and email some scripts to clients. If you've properly spelled out the instructions, there should be little, if any, guesswork involved on their part.

But if you're in a bad shape, the last thing you want to add to your family's worries is taking care of your business. In this case, the emergency plan executor ideally would be a VA or another business assistant or associate. You can also ask a trusted colleague or a close friend.

Your emergency contact would still need to reach out to the executor, so make sure they at least know of each other if they're not acquainted.

For my emergency contact, I keep a file labeled something like "in the case of major emergency" on my main computer's desktop, and I email the doc to the person when I update it periodically or leave town for a few days.

In this document, I describe the procedures to get things rolling, the location of the SOPs, and any other pertinent details for the executor.

Your Quick To-Do Checklist for Setting Up Processes

Now:

✓ Payment terms and invoice template

✓ Expense tracking system/app

Now or later:

✓ Computer security and backup

✓ Project workflow system/app

✓ Client onboarding and offboarding checklist

Later:

✓ Marketing SOPs

✓ Emergency business SOPs

Get your step-by-step cheat sheet with all four components together broken down by tiers at freelancerscompass.com/cheatsheet.

Spotlight on: Scott Stransky

Business name: Full Funnel Content
Location: Denver, Colorado
Founded: October 2009
Business structure: LLC
Website: funnelcontent.com

Scott Stransky's agency, Full Funnel Content, provides content writing for B2B technology companies. The business employs a remote team of four employees, in addition to several contracted writers.

Scott's career began in sales and client services before he transitioned to writing customer case studies for very well-known global tech brands. While he took a detour from writing to open his own gym, he returned to writing after three years — but stayed on his own instead of returning to a corporate life. For six years, he grew his new business more than 60% year over year, subcontracting some of the writing to his friends before fully embracing an agency in 2019.

What was your biggest challenge when you first got started?

Finding clients was one of them. I didn't have a marketing program or budget and really didn't know how or where to find clients outside of asking former co-workers and friends. So, I tapped into my sales experiences and figured out the easiest way to identify "qualified" leads was by scouring the job boards.

If a company posts a job in the same vein as what I do — whether it's actually the same work or the manager of the person doing that work — it's almost guaranteed they have the budget, need, and the timeline for filling the job.

I then began to map out how corporate marketing departments are segmented, who does what, and how many different layers and levels of leadership there are, and used that to target messaging at the ones responsible for the vacant position. Then, I replicated it across the different mini-functions within the marketing department.

What was the biggest surprise about going from a corporate career to running a business?

The biggest surprise happened in reverse. It is shocking how much faster the pace of running a business is than working in corporate. I had a boss once tell me that a project I could do in literally 24 hours wasn't due for a month.

It was just unfathomable to me as a writer and a doer that there was such a lack of a sense of urgency. Running a business is all urgency. You're ultimately responsible for the success or failure of the business. You're responsible for making sure it makes money. So, there's always this sense of doing more, more, more — faster, faster, faster!

What is one thing you wish you knew when you switched from a corporate path?

I really wish I had had a better understanding of taxes and accounting for small businesses. There are so many complexities and nuances to both that can either cost you or save you a lot of money. I wish I had known it was going to be such a pain and that I'd sought help learning what I needed to know.

What do you attribute your business success to?

Perseverance and fearlessness. Being self-employed is hard. Being self-employed while employing others — being directly responsible for other people's (and their families) financial well-being — is even harder. It's not for everyone. But you can't be afraid of that responsibility, nor can you be afraid of failing.

I have a lot of ideas — some big ones, others that may be off the wall to some people. I pursue them with as much energy and tenacity as I can muster to make them happen, knowing full well that they may not work out. And I have to be okay with that potential outcome and have the willingness to either see it through to its conclusion or to pivot and try something else.

What's your best advice to someone making or contemplating the switch?

Be prepared to fail. Regardless of how much you study, survey, and prepare, you're going to make mistakes, and you'll make a lot of them. It's part of the process.

What's next for you?

Continue building our agency into something bigger, stronger, and more resilient (and more profitable). Possibly spinning off an AI-based tool we're working on internally into a new AI-oriented company.

Chapter 5

Tools and Support Systems

(Loose) category definition: Any resources — technology (e.g., apps and digital services), human (e.g., professional service providers, assistants), and knowledge (e.g., training programs, associations) — that make your job and work life easier

> *The ability to simplify means to eliminate the unnecessary so that the necessary may speak."*
>
> *— Hans Hofman*

First, a special note about generative AI tools like ChatGPT. I'd be amiss if I didn't mention the hottest trend since the Macarena.

I left out recommendations not because I don't think these tools are useful, but because I haven't implemented them enough to figure out how to optimize the operations side of the business with genAI. And, more importantly, genAI's capabilities are changing so rapidly that by the time you read this book, my tips will likely be outdated.

I pay for the latest ChatGPT version, and I've used it for things like research, brainstorming business ideas, and writing a funny bio. It's a great tool for sparking my creating thinking when I'm stuck. I've used Perplexity for research. Etc. But I haven't taken the time — yet — to find the best way for operationalizing genAI tools so I can run the business side better.

That said, I encourage you to experiment with the genAI apps that interest you to make your operations more efficient. As long as they complement — rather than distract from — what you should really be doing to build a foundation for your business. You don't want to be left behind by the genAI wave, but you also don't want to get so excited about it that you ignore your real work.

Tier 1

Professional email address

I consider a professional email address a Tier 1 item.

But I know you can Gmail or Yahoo your way to successful delivery with no problem (and maybe even Hotmail it, but that's really pushing it). Plus, it may take time to decide on a business name and URL, and you don't need this step to be your excuse to not get started.

So, as long as you don't mind hunting for business messages among emails with sales specials from Target, newsletters from Auntie Sarah, and daily digests from *Mashable* or *The Onion*, you do you.

However, some prospects won't take you seriously without a professional email address.

Nor would you want to publish your personal email online, and eventually you'll have to list your business contact info somewhere because if you don't have any professional footprint online, you just look sketch.

Speaking for myself, I would never hire a vendor or freelancer who doesn't have an online presence or only communicates through a free email account or third-party services like LinkedIn, Slack, Signal, or whatever.

Maybe your prospects aren't that picky. But do you really want to entrust your business success to a free email service, no matter how reliable it may be?

Pro Tip

There are various ways to create a professional email like yourname@yourbusinessname.com without having a live website. You just need to buy a domain (URL) and "park" it until you're ready to build a website.

For example, if you buy a subscription to Office 365 or Google Workspace (which you'll want to do at some point), you can either use Microsoft as your email server or create email aliases in Workspace.

Another possibility is your domain host, which may offer an email service for free or a small monthly fee.

Word-processing apps

If your deliverable is content, it goes without saying that you'll need a word-processing app like Microsoft Word or Google Docs to create and submit your work.

If you don't have a current version of Microsoft Office, you can get away with free Google Docs for a while. But eventually, you'll likely have to bite the bullet and subscribe to Office 365.

Your clients will likely accept your delivery in Google Docs, but some will then submit their feedback to you as Word attachments. No biggie; you can upload that back to Google for revisions (and continue this cycle ad nauseam).

Sooner or later, you'll get tired of this game of yo-yo. You may also run into some formatting issues. And let me tell you, going through a draft like a 3,500-word whitepaper to delete wonky formatting manually is nobody's dream.

Personally, I don't recommend relying on the free version of Google Workspace anyway, and not just because I have trust issues with tech companies. (Yes, I know I work in tech.)

No matter how much confidence you have in Google, storing all your work in Drive means you're entrusting the single copy of your documents to a tech giant doing you a free favor. (What can go wrong, right?)

Plus, if you're working from some exciting place like your sailboat or a remote village in Tibet, you'll cry every time you need to access your online-only doc. (Yes, the Google Drive desktop app is a workaround; go for it if you don't have any Big Tech trust issues like I do.)

Time tracking app

Time tracking? Say what? Didn't you rejoice just a few chapters ago that you don't need to punch the clock anymore?

It's true: If you're a writer, like me, you can take your sweet time to do research until your fingers turn blue, agonize over every sentence, and make every deliverable your masterpiece.

If that's your jam, however, you should be a poet or novel writer because creating strategy or content at that poetic speed will earn you just as little money but a lot less fame.

But seriously. Whatever field you're in, if you were paid by the hour at your job or your employer rewarded busywork so you were in no hurry to reach the finish line, you'll soon learn new rules of the game.

If you're smart (which I know you are since you're reading this book) and charging flat fees, the faster you work, the more you'll earn hour-per-hour. This doesn't mean cutting corners and delivering subpar products. It simply means learning how to be more efficient at every task and knowing how to price your work appropriately.

All this to say: Keep track of your time so you know how long each type of service or deliverable takes you to execute.

This includes everything from the kickoff meeting and client communications to the project management and the actual work.

Once you've delivered several similar projects, you'll have a general idea of how much effort goes into a specific type of deliverable. In addition to helping with pricing, this data is necessary for setting realistic delivery timelines.

Don't stop at tracking client time. Track everything you do during the workday, including admin, marketing, and business management tasks.

A clear picture of what's eating up your time will come in handy for various purposes, whether you're looking to outsource specific tasks or trying to identify where you need to improve efficiency. Especially if you love going down the rabbit hole that is social media (for work purposes, of course!).

After all this time in business, I still run a tracker every day, using the free app Clockify (see Chapter 8 for more suggestions). I'm running one right now for a task called "Open to Work book" (the original working title of this book), grouped under my company name as the "client."

To give you an idea of other nMeta Communications activities I track, here's a sampling of the tasks:

- BizDev (which has subtasks like strategy, Monday check-ins, and business retreats — more on both of these later in this chapter)
- Marketing (LinkedIn, website, follow-ups)
- Admin (client onboarding, client negotiations, planning)
- Email (I probably don't want to know)

If you ask me how long I spend on a task like project management every week, I can log into Clockify and tell you in a few seconds.

My VA archives Clockify reports monthly for me so I can reference them any time. The data has been useful on numerous occasions when I needed to know how long it takes me to create certain types of deliverables.

Tier 2

Other essential apps

If you're a marketer, you may appreciate the slogan, "There's an app for that." I'm not advocating adopting this motto as a wholesale approach to managing your business.

There are oodles of productivity and other apps that promise to make your job smoother. (We, marketers, know — we write that messaging!) The trick is to make sure the apps are actually saving you time, tedious work, or some other frustration.

When a task takes far too long or seems unnecessarily complicated, it may be time for a new tool. You'll find your own sweet spot for when to stop doing things on paper or manually. I'm offering a few ideas for consideration in the meantime.

These can be Tier 2 or Tier 3, depending on how soon you find yourself in need of more sanity.

Scheduling

If you love offering a personal touch for scheduling client meetings, enjoy that eureka feeling when you finally land on a time after all those back-and-forth emails.

When you're having to schedule dozens of them every month, that white-glove model quickly becomes unruly. Especially if you want to avoid double booking or starting the loop over when someone needs to reschedule.

With a scheduling app (I use the paid version of Calendly), you'll set up your availability once, sync your calendar, send the link to clients or prospects, and just kick back and wait for appointments to make themselves.

(Just kidding. You have to work really hard at marketing for that. But hey, you can invest the time saved through automated scheduling back into marketing; win-win!)

Project management

Paper calendars and to-do lists are awesome for keeping track of deadlines and tasks. And not just because I'm GenX and apps weren't a thing in my early career. Who doesn't love the satisfying feeling of crossing things off a list? With a real pen?

Excel (or Google Sheets, if you must) works great, too, for tracking current projects and archiving old ones over time. If you like your bells and whistles, free versions of apps like Trello, Asana, and Notability offer extra perks like reminders and some other automation.

I'm not pushing you in either direction, but I'll say this: An app that syncs to all your devices can be a lifesaver if you take advantage of your freedom to work from wherever you darn please.

I prefer Trello for my own project management (paid version for extra functionality), but many of my clients onboard me onto their own platforms, typically Asana.

And — this may shock you, sorry! — I also use Excel (including a separate "bandwidth" calendar to make sure I don't overbook projects), a monthly hard copy calendar for deadlines, and a weekly planner with pages I tear off at the end of each week (Oh, the bliss!).

Overkill? Probably.

Unnecessary duplication? For some things, yes. I didn't claim to be a productivity expert, did I? But this system works for me.

I have my synced Trello boards on all my four work-related devices, I (securely) share my Excel tracker with my bookkeeper, I love seeing my deadlines on a monthly printed sheet, and I absolutely need a daily to-do list that I can physically cross off.

Did I forget to mention I list my projects monthly on a whiteboard, too? (Have you tried the experience of erasing completed projects at the end of a month? Highly recommended.)

Accounting

As I noted in Chapter 2, you'll want to go beyond a simple expense-tracking system like Excel (or a shoebox) at some point.

You can use a tracking app like Expensify, but I recommend a more comprehensive bookkeeping tool that has additional functionalities such as invoicing.

Or skip the app and go straight to outsourcing your bookkeeping. I recommend that farther down in Tier 3, but you may be ready much sooner.

You'll know when you're ready for a bookkeeper because you'll love this task so much, you'll postpone it until tax time — so you can attach yourself to your computer for several weekends and relish the data-entry marathon. True story (the marathon, not the relishing part).

Templates

I mentioned templates throughout the other chapters, but I'm adding them as a separate item here to bring it all together.

Templates can fall into any tier, and I'm labeling them as Tier 2 somewhat randomly and somewhat logically: By this point, you should already have some of them in place and consider adding others.

Templates are your ticket to optimizing your time and improving productivity. What else is there to say?

Following is a sample list of what kind of templates you can — and should eventually — create. Note that I'm including some templates for marketing in addition to operations because I view templatizing as part of streamlining your BizOps.

You can templatize:

- Proposals
- Invoices
- Client contracts
- Vendor contracts (e.g., VAs, writers)
- SoWs
- Prospecting emails/LinkedIn messages
- Replies to inbound inquiries (for various scenarios)
- Follow-up emails to dormant or former clients
- Discovery session questions
- New client onboarding/welcome emails
- Client project management or deliverables workflows
- Project kickoff questions
- Requests for testimonials

Security apps

Indulge me one more time as I put my cybersecurity writer hat on for another second.

Security has three components: people, processes, and technology (tools). The people component includes you and any of your support staff, and I've covered some tips about people and processes in Chapter 4.

As far as tech, I recommend doing a few things beyond the typical antivirus to protect your data (and your business and clients).

At the risk of sounding redundant, remember that I'm not a cyber-security expert; I only play one in my marketing lane. Meaning, I have more knowledge than the average consumer or businessperson, but I am not a trained cyber expert with hands-on expertise in fighting the bad guys.

So, just like my accounting and legal tips, view this list as a starting point to give you an idea of what to look for. For more in-depth knowledge, consider bartering your awesome marketing (or?) skills for a consult with an IT/security expert specializing in small businesses.

For the curious bunch, I mention the tools I use specifically, but this is not an endorsement by any means (nor do I get any kickbacks).

VPN (virtual private network)

An absolute must-have if you use public Wi-Fi, even password-protected Wi-Fi at places like hotels and libraries. I've used Private Internet Access for years and haven't had any issues with it. Many router firewalls (see below) offer a built-in VPN as well.

Password manager

Another must-have to help you create and store strong, unique passwords. Many now also store passkeys, the newest authentication tool. I use Dashlane and love it (and not just because I've been writing for Dashlane for a few years).

DNS security

This tool protects your computer from connecting to malicious websites, such as phishing sites or sites infected with malware. I've been using OpenDNS (a lighter version of Cisco Umbrella) and am happy with it for the most part. I also use Plume to optimize Wi-Fi in our very big house, and Plume has built-in DNS protection.

Endpoint protection

While consumer-grade antivirus software is technically endpoint (computer) protection, an upgrade to a business-level solution will give you a leg up, even if it's a basic one. I've used Acronis, Sophos, and Bitdefender at different times, as they had solopreneur-friendly plans, but some beefed-up consumer versions may also offer you what you need.

Router firewall

Many routers come with built-in firewalls, but they're not turned on by default. You'll need to do a little homework to figure out if yours has one and how to enable it. You can also buy a separate hardware appliance or install a software one. (Sophos, for example, offers a free one for home use on Intel-compatible PCs as of this writing.)

Multifactor authentication (MFA)

While not foolproof by any means, MFA adds extra protection to your online accounts. Use an authenticator app instead of having codes texted or emailed to you, when possible. I've used Duo (acquired by Cisco a few years ago) for some time and love it. But I have a cautionary tale: If you have to switch your mobile device, you need to prep for the transition in advance because restoring accounts in Duo is a pain otherwise.

Peer networking groups

Although I'm labeling this as Tier 2, I recommend making this a priority as soon as you're done setting up the basics, if not before.

Don't simply view your peers as competition, even if they are. Rather, think of them as an invaluable resource.

Other freelancers and business owners, whether at the same stage as you or more experienced, can be your support network, advisers, and cheerleaders all rolled into one.

Facebook groups, Slack groups, Zoom networking groups — they come in different flavors, and are not always free. Regardless of the format, they offer an excellent opportunity to learn from others like you, ask for advice and recommendations, share experiences, and even get project leads and referrals.

Finding the right group for you may take some time, and you can always start your own. I did that recently for high-earning marketing freelancers because I wanted to compare notes on how and what others are doing.

One way to find people who may be interested is by networking on LinkedIn and building relationships with a few peers whose career you admire or is similar to yours.

Accountability partners

An offshoot from peer networking groups (and also a candidate for Tier 1), accountability partners are a much smaller and more focused version of networking. The main goal is to help keep each other on track, but accountability partners can become much more.

Remember my "Monday check-ins" Clockify task? That's for my weekly accountability buddies, Mary and Diane.

We've been meeting virtually on Mondays for the past six years, supporting each other personally and professionally. We were paired up as part of an income accelerator program that freelance writer and coach Carol Tice offered once upon a time.

The three of us have been meeting faithfully every week since then, with some exceptions now and then when unavoidable interruptions come up. We make ourselves unavailable for any other meetings during those one or two hours. (Our record was three hours once.) One year, we even met on Saturdays as well for four hours of co-working with a focus on marketing and business development.

Although we're scattered across the country, we've become good friends (Diane and I even met in person finally!). I owe my two

Monday buddies a lot for not only helping me grow my business but also encouraging me to pursue other things (like my art or this book).

(Shout-out to Carol Tice here; while she's no longer involved with that accelerator program, you can learn about her or reach out through caroltice.com.)

I also had an accountability buddy for this book. (Here's to Nicci! Thanks for nudging me along!)

There's no better way to light a fire under you than an upcoming accountability meeting where you'll be reporting for the third week in a row that you haven't done a thing. I promise you'll be motivated in no time — if only to save face.

Pro Tip

Industry associations are another great way of networking, not just with peers but often with potential clients.

The best organizations offer a range of benefits such as events, member-only educational resources, and databases listing members' services.

My experience has been mixed with membership associations, which is not to say they're not a good resource.

Look for those that are active, have local chapters or events if you prefer in-person networking, and offer membership perks that are truly valuable for you.

And then be active — visibility is key to attracting opportunities.

Digital portfolio

This is another item that is borderline Tier 1. You'll need it to land clients unless you're working with someone who already knows your skills well, like former co-workers and partners.

However, a portfolio may take some time to put together, especially if you have an NDA, don't have immediate access to your previous work, or created documents like content strategy or marketing messaging that were classified as confidential.

You may need to ask permission from your former employer to use your work in your portfolio (since technically, all that work was "for hire" and you don't have the right to publish or share it if it's not already publicly accessible).

Again, you don't want this step to be a hang-up, but I recommend you get working on it right away.

Start by collecting work samples and organizing them (By industry? Asset type? Or some other way that makes more sense to your target audience?) so you don't have to spend a lot of time hunting for them.

If you don't have a website yet, find a free portfolio site (see Chapter 8) that serves your purpose in the meantime and create a profile there.

When a prospect asks for examples, don't just send the portfolio link. Instead, send curated links to a handful of samples that reflect the type of project they are looking for, the type of industry they're in, or anything else that's as similar to their project as you have.

Ideally, even PDFs should be sent as links instead of attachments because some people prefer that. Not to mention that assets like e-books are often not optimized for email, and you don't want to send multiple ginormous files.

Pro Tip

If you have content published on websites, create a PDF of that page and save it. I can't tell you how many times my work has disappeared online because the client redid the website, took down old content, or (occasionally) went out of business or closed the channel.

My VA makes PDFs of my new work as soon as it's published, and I store them in folders created for each client on my hard drive (backed up to the cloud).

This has been a lifesaver on several occasions when I wanted to share a relevant example that's no longer live or an article link in my portfolio had disappeared from the client's website (in which case I can upload the archived PDF to my website and link to the PDF instead).

My VA also maintains a shared spreadsheet with sheets for each website or brand and the links to the published work, so I can quickly look up specific content by client.

TIER 3

Bookkeeping

If you get to Tier 3 and haven't hired a bookkeeper yet, stop reading and go do that. Right now.

By this point, you should be delegating things that are, to borrow a phrase from people smarter than me, "not in your zone of genius." And — unless you missed your calling or dropped out of accounting school by accident — bookkeeping is probably not your top talent.

Bookkeeping should be one of the first things to go when you're ready to take tasks off your plate. If you hire the right person, your bookkeeper will save you from yourself — in terms of both time and mistakes.

A word of caution: Once you congratulate yourself for hiring a bookkeeper, don't reach for the champagne just yet.

Outsourcing this task doesn't mean your days of profit-and-loss statements are over (I know, way to ruin the mood!). As with any business function, you'll need to continue doing your due diligence — which means auditing your books regularly, keeping track of your numbers, and so forth.

Professional development

If you've attended work conferences, you already know they're one of the best ways to learn, keep up with your industry trends, network, etc. And who doesn't love an all-expenses-paid time away from deadlines?

Continuing with the theme of ruined moods, let me remind you that nobody is going to pay you to get away from deliverables for a few hours or days and learn new things.

What this means is that you'll have to be even more proactive to attend these events — budgeting both time and money in advance. Since you're the big boss and all that, you have to put your foot down and make this non-optional.

Whether you've been in business for 30 days or 30 years, continuing education is vital. Even more vital when you own a business and you're tired of going to the school of hard knocks.

Professional development can be as simple as a one-hour free webinar on developing your business brand and as involved as a full-week, in-person industry conference or a 12-month business development course.

The point is that you absolutely need to keep learning if you want to stay competitive, make more money, and do more than simply survive.

Pro Tip

You need to be smart about your money and time spent on professional development.

The opportunities for learning are truly unlimited, both free and paid. That makes it very easy to fall into the trap of spending hours and hours in various sessions until you have no brain cells left, then never implement a single takeaway.

It's just as easy to pay for program after program and give up midway or not use it at all. Been there more times than I care to admit — so feel free to learn from my mistakes.

Best advice I can give is:

• **Be selective.**

Make sure the course, program, conference, etc. is focused on an area you truly want or need to learn about at this point in time. Promotional content for these offerings can be very enticing and sound good in the moment. But your enthusiasm may wane by the time the event rolls in, especially if your incentive to sign up was the fear of missing out.

• **Be committed.**

If you're going to sign up for something, make sure you schedule time to debrief yourself and think of ways to implement any of the useful things you learned.

Even if the session or program doesn't cost you money, you're still spending your precious time on it. Free doesn't mean no cost; the cost is your time.

If you're just going to multitask while half-listening, you might as well watch YouTube while folding laundry, dusting your house, or filing. You'll learn just as little, but at least your multitasking will result in a cleaner space.

• Be skeptical.

Far too many people who make a living as content creators overpromise and underdeliver.

The internet is littered with courses that are nothing but poorly edited recordings of a live program offered long ago, or programs where the advertised outcomes are an exception rather than the norm.

Read the fine print (especially if you're looking to spend a lot of money), poke around, ask questions. Be an educated consumer.

My pet peeve is sales pitches disguised as free webinars. Don't get me wrong, I'm not against webinars that pitch a product or brand. As a marketing professional, I know they have a place in the marketing and sales funnel. The ones that irk me are those that are advertised as educational content and give you three bullet points' worth of useful info.

Be as smart about your time as you are about your money. Understand that many webinars are going to sell you something, and if you're prone to impulse shopping or have a hard time saying no, you're likely to walk away learning very little while throwing money at yet another program or course that you may never complete.

As one of my coaches told me, most people never take full advantage of the things they pay for, if they use them at all. Don't be those people.

Mentors and coaches

Speaking of coaches. While they're last on my list of support systems, they're certainly not least. Like accountability buddies and peer networking groups, great coaches and mentors are worth their weight in gold. I include them in Tier 3 mostly because coaches, and often mentors as well, are a financial investment — and possibly not a small one.

Notice I used the word investment and not expense. It's a subtle nuance: You're spending money, but this money will help you make more money in the long run (assuming you've picked a good coach).

That said, there are many resources for finding wonderful mentors and coaches who will work with you at no charge. I mention a few in Chapter 8.

Of course, you can always reach out directly to other seasoned entrepreneurs for advice.

If you're looking for a long-term relationship rather than one-time advice, however, be transparent upfront. Ask these individuals if they're open to mentoring you. Some may simply be too overwhelmed with their own business to afford the time, but perhaps would be gracious to answer a few specific questions. (See pro tip below on how to "pick someone's brain.")

Pro Tip

Many successful, experienced professionals (including me) are happy to pay it forward by sharing what they know. But we are all busy people with our own businesses to grow.

You'll never get a reply (from me at least) if you randomly message me on LinkedIn and ask me if I have any advice for a freelancer getting started in cybersecurity.

Of course I have advice. Lots of it.

But I'm going to simply delete that message.

I'm not going to help anyone who is too lazy to think of a thoughtful question and doesn't know how to start a conversation that comes with an ask.

And I'm definitely not going to have coffee with someone who just tells me they want to "pick my brain" about XYZ.

Each professional will react differently to the ask, so I'm speaking for myself only here.

But I'm willing to bet you'll get other people's attention using an approach similar to this:

• Briefly introduce yourself. One sentence! Two if they're short. Period.

• Tell me what you want (my advice) and why you think I'm the right person to give it to you.

• Don't forget to mention if we met somewhere (I likely won't remember) or you heard me speak at a specific event.

• Ask if I'm open to answering a couple of questions and then list those questions. (Don't send a laundry list of questions; choose your most important ones.)

This not only saves me time and brain cells from having a back-and-forth with you, but also gives me an idea of the kind of commitment I'm looking at, timewise.

• Follow up. But only once.

I may have meant to respond and forgot, and your follow-up will get you back on my radar.

But if you pinged me twice and heard crickets, that's your answer — I'm not up for it.

I do my best to acknowledge people who are thoughtful in their ask, but something may be going on in my personal or professional life that's consuming all my focus.

Don't be discouraged if one more person doesn't get back to you.

As long as you're mindful and respectful about it, knock on more doors. I promise you that some will open.

If you received answers and are burning to add more questions, ask in your thank-you message if that's a possibility.

Make it clear if it's just a one-time follow-up or you're hoping to send more questions occasionally. Again, be specific with your ask and realistic about your expectations.

By the way, a similarly direct approach works well for networking one-on-one with your peers.

If you want to have a virtual or in-person meeting to compare notes with someone in the same niche, in a complementary field, and so on, let them know why you're reaching out, what you're looking to get out of the conversation, and how it will benefit you both.

Start with one meeting, and if you hit it off, explore together the idea of doing it monthly, quarterly, or even just occasionally.

The relationships that come out of these spontaneous beginnings can truly blossom and prove invaluable for your career.

Self-sponsored business retreats

Once you make your way through coaches and business development programs, you'll likely come across the idea of business retreats. These are one-off events that bring together other entrepreneurs for several days' worth of workshops, networking, and working on their businesses.

Those are definitely worth considering and are excellent tools to help you uplevel.

What I'm talking about here, though, is something else.

Self-sponsored business retreats are your personal "getaways" for a few days away from the daily routines. Except instead of recharging and relaxing, you're spending time on business development.

I've been doing business retreats for several years, and they're one of my favorite tools for growing my business. They're an excellent way to give yourself time and space for deep work — not on your clients' projects, but on your own.

I typically book a hotel room or a vacation rental some driving distance away from home. It's similar to the idea of having a separate space for my work — I'm designating a place for a business function, which helps me get into the right headspace.

You can do a business retreat at your home or office, of course, and save a few hundred dollars.

For me, being away eliminates all the client and domestic distractions. I am also motivated to get the work done — I don't feel like wasting the money I paid for accommodations.

I've had retreats as short as two days and as long as a week. I would do that quarterly if I had my druthers, but realistically, I can usually only pull off one or two a year.

Regardless of their frequency, they're typically very productive, and I come away energized and inspired.

Here's how I organize them:

- Plan far in advance — ideally at least two to three months — working around any set deadlines, like my recurring production times for the magazines I edit or design.

- Choose a place that looks comfortable and has space for me to spread out, and make the reservations. A microwave, fridge, coffee pot, and seating area like a couch are prerequisite. So is free internet. A view is nice, but I find that I rarely take advantage of it. I don't like to drive longer than about an hour, so typically I'm within 60 miles or so from home.

- Inform clients about OOO (out-of-office) dates as I would about any time off. Block the days off in my calendar. Make sure to add OOO email autoresponders when the time comes so I don't feel obligated to answer emails (because I most certainly will not).

- Start a board in Trello with potential agenda items as ideas come up during my daily activities.

- Set the agenda a few days ahead of the event, organized by day, with approximate time blocks designated to each specific task and any relevant links I'll need, such as articles or videos.

- Include a final task that involves "debriefing" myself and creating an action list for the next few months.

- Get a little shopping done on my way to the location or in the neighborhood for snacks and quick lunches to minimize disruptions (and the expense of food delivery services).

I tend to work 10–12 hours a day during these retreats because once I'm on a roll, it's hard to quit. Even so, I never get through everything on the list, even if I spend five days holed up in a hotel room, because the agenda is usually crammed.

I also build in a little time to decompress — take a couple of hours to read a book, visit a local bookstore, or just stream a show on my iPad.

Here are just a few things I've done on my business retreats:

- Brainstormed names for my rebranded business.

- Caught up on replays for past conferences and other events I signed up for.

- Reviewed and revised my marketing plan.

- Read through the dozens of open tabs with saved articles on marketing, business, and other topics of interest, and jotted down ideas for action.

- Spent time on overdue admin tasks (which, admittedly, may not be the best retreat activity, but it's perfect for late evening when my brain is fried yet I'm not ready to stop).

Recap

Your Quick To-Do Checklist for Setting Up Support Systems

Now:

- ✓ URL/email address
- ✓ Time-tracking app
- ✓ Word-processing app
- ✓ Digital portfolio

Now or later:

- ✓ Scheduling and project-management apps
- ✓ Bookkeeping system or support
- ✓ Peer support and networking group
- ✓ Cybersecurity
- ✓ Coach or mentor

Later:

- ✓ Templates
- ✓ Virtual assistant
- ✓ Accountability partner
- ✓ Professional development

Spotlight on: Divya Agrawal

Business name: DA Creative Web Services (OPC) Pvt Lt
Location: Madhya Pradesh, India
Founded: November 2018
Business structure: Sole proprietor
Website: freelancetechwriter.com

Divya Agrawal is a freelance B2B technology writer specializing in long-form content such as whitepapers, case studies, thought leadership, and knowledge-base articles. She has worked with more than 60 B2B technology companies in the AI, Internet of Things, blockchain, Web3, cybersecurity, AI operations (AIOps), and development operations (DevOps) sectors. A software engineering graduate, she worked as a Salesforce developer for a year before switching to a career in writing.

Divya got her first clients as a referral from a family member's company and has consistently scaled her business until entering a period of personal turmoil. She is now rebuilding the business better than ever, with the goal of upleveling and hitting a six-figure income.

What was the biggest surprise about going from a corporate career to running a business?

This is something I still feel intensely: No one tells you what to do. If you sleep in the whole day and do nothing, you aren't answerable or accountable to anyone as long as you meet client deadlines. This means you have to grow up and take accountability for your own life and business really fast. And, you have to keep the momentum going when you hit a slump. It all starts and ends with you.

What was your biggest mistake in terms of operations, and how did you fix it?

I wouldn't call it my biggest mistake, but it was a naive approach to freelancing. The way I was taking on clients in my first year of freelancing. I had 10 clients who all agreed to my rates (could've been my clue to raise my rates). I was nearing burnout, and that woke me up. It took me a while to define my positioning, say no when a client wasn't a good fit, and realize that admin work multiplies with each client.

Now, I only take on three to four clients at a time. I fixed the problem by raising my rates, dropping clients who couldn't afford me anymore, and better planning my time. I scheduled space for recreation and rest to prevent burnout.

What do you attribute your business success to?

I believe that your business and personal growth go hand in hand. So, if you stay stuck with limiting beliefs personally, it reflects in your business. Once I started working on myself, my personal life shifted and my business shifted. I don't tie my worth to my revenue anymore (while believing my work is high-quality and worth my rates) and don't take feedback personally, among other things. It's really interesting how emotional and psychological maturity can make you a better business owner.

What's your one piece of advice to someone making or contemplating the switch?

Get a community! I can't recommend it enough. I was a member of Carol Tice's Freelance Writers Den for three years and it was so valuable to me in figuring out freelancing. Currently, I don't recommend the Den though, as Carol sold it and it's not the same since. But I'm part of Mandy Ellis' Wealth Lab community. I took her course and joined it afterward.

I cannot stress enough the power of having like-minded people around you, no matter what community you find. You learn a lot just by seeing how others run their business, the challenges they overcome, the way they write, and how others do all the stuff that comes with the territory.

What has been the best part about the path you've chosen as a business owner?

The best part for me is being able to dictate my time and energy. My business was a blessing to me when my life was a struggle. I faced mental health challenges and lost interest in everything, but never let go of my business. It became my purpose and my support system when I wanted to distract myself from my personal life.

I took time off when I needed to and had enough savings to make it through a challenging year. That's the most important part of it to me. That my business came through when I needed it to. I know that my friends were facing layoff possibilities at the same time.

What's next for you?

I'm focusing on improving my editing skills right now and learning by observing and reading a lot. I follow the greats in the field. I've raised my rates and am on my way to earning more and delivering better work. That's what I focus on, and earning $10K/month would just be a welcome side effect.

Chapter 6

Roadmap

(Loose) category definition: A plan (or multiple plans) stating your goals, vision, objectives, strategies, and other aspects that help you stay on track.

> Alice: "Would you tell me, please, which way I ought to go from here?"
>
> The Cheshire Cat: "That depends a good deal on where you want to get to."
>
> Alice: "I don't much care where."
>
> The Cheshire Cat: "Then it doesn't much matter which way you go."
>
> Alice: ". . . so long as I get somewhere."
>
> The Cheshire Cat: "Oh, you're sure to do that, if only you walk long enough."
>
> — Lewis Carroll, Alice in Wonderland

This chapter is different from the ones discussing infrastructure, processes, and tools in that I am not assigning tiers to the various components. Instead, I'll cover briefly the why and the how.

Roadmapping, technically, falls outside of "business operations." But I'm diving into it at a high level so you can see how everything ties together.

(Note: If you're a linear-thinking person, you may want to do your roadmap before you dive into anything else.)

The Why

Simply put, you should have a roadmap at the beginning of your entrepreneurial journey, which makes the entire thing Tier 1. In the ideal world.

In reality, you'll likely spend all your energy for a while on setting up shop and finding work.

You won't know where you're going to be in a month or two, let alone in a year or five. Creating a roadmap at this stage feels like a lot of added pressure. Besides, it's a guessing game.

But.

Without a vision or goal — and at least a general idea of what you'll do to get there — growing your business will always feel like a lot of pressure.

You'll meander from one project to the next, take any project that comes along, and have no idea where your income will land at the end of each year.

I know this because that was my path for many years in business.

I didn't have any clear financial goals, a true vision for my business and career, or a good understanding of my ideal or target customers (by now, you know that "anyone who pays" is not a niche).

Consequently, I didn't have very good processes for getting and managing quality clients. I ran my business haphazardly, which is a generous description because I didn't think of myself as a business owner in the true sense of the word.

After all, if you're just letting your business happen to you, do you really "own" it?

Building your business without a roadmap is like taking a trip to a new destination without GPS.

You'll get there eventually.

But how much longer and more expensive will your trip be? How about your stress levels as you're going in circles in search of the right streets?

(Yes, I'm old enough to remember traveling with a paper map or handwritten directions. We managed. Wanna go back to those days? I didn't think so.)

Yes, But ...

All that said, I'll throw another idea at you. As long as you don't think of it as an excuse not to seek clarity for what you want and are trying to do.

I recently read *Risk Forward* by Victoria Labalme and was intrigued by her approach to gaining clarity. Essentially, she advocates for the opposite of planning and goal setting, and rather "embracing the unknown" and figuring out things by doing it.

This approach goes against everything we're taught and believe in our business, professional, and personal lives. It's audacious and provocative — but it has merit.

Besides, the word Audacia in my DBAs comes from the word audacious in Latin, so I would never tell someone to discount audacious ideas.

I'm not advocating for abandoning the traditional way and using Labalme's approach as a way out of roadmapping. I'm simply keeping an open mind and suggesting you do the same as you figure out what's best for you.

If you're still with me on this and believe having a GPS, or at least a compass, is the best route for you (no pun intended), read the rest of the chapter for the roadmapping "how."

Otherwise, see you in Chapter 7.

Suggested Roadmapping Steps

Like I wrote at the beginning of this book, a roadmap can be as simple or detailed as you want.

Either way, plan to spend some uninterrupted time on it. You'll need to think deeply about what you want, why you want it, and how you'll go about it.

I recommend at least three components for your roadmap.

1. Your vision

What do you want for yourself and your business? At a minimum, include a paragraph that states what you hope to achieve.

My vision "statement" — which I review roughly biannually — has 17 bullet points, adapted from recommendations I received from career coach Angee Linsey.

These bullets cover everything from who my "colleagues" are and what my work environment (home office) looks like, to how much I'm earning, what gives me satisfaction, and what I'm still missing in my professional life.

You don't need this kind of a page-long manifesto — just some clarity about your 10,000-foot view of your business.

I'll say this: The first time I wrote in my vision that I'm earning $120–150K a year, I laughed out loud at how preposterous that sounded.

I broke the six-figure barrier that year and have stayed on course since then.

(A shout-out to Angee — who knew that vision statement would hold so much power! She now offers the vision exercise for free through her coaching website, daretobedeliberate.com, so I highly encourage you to check it out.)

This is not about implementing some sort of mystical "manifest your wishes to the universe" type practice.

(Though there's nothing wrong with doing that if that's how you roll).

I'm simply saying that once you put things in writing, you have a much better understanding of what you want from your entrepreneurial path.

2. Your business goals

Goal is a broad term, and you can interpret it your own way. Consider having a short, strategic list with longer-term goals and a more detailed list for your annual goals. Either way, keep it simple.

To give you some inspiration, here's what I had for my 2023 goals:

- Increase revenues (not achieved, which is okay, given the market conditions).

- Add another stream of income to diversify (not achieved per se, but I put the wheels in motion).

- Continue to mature my business and find efficiencies (work in progress).

- Develop book to write for 2024. (Yay! Here I am. I actually forgot this was on my 2023 goals list until I revisited it while writing this section. As I stated earlier, when you write things down, it may seem weird how stuff "just happens." Which is not to say you shouldn't periodically review your goals throughout the year to remind yourself what you're working toward.)

- What I want to stop doing, start doing, and continue doing; and what I want to do more of and less of (three bullets each — a shout-out to Ilise Benun for the idea).

3. Your income objectives

How much do you need or want to earn? Again, don't overthink it. Just give yourself a ballpark so you can keep an eye on your cash flow and know when you need to step up marketing to meet your minimums. Don't forget to account for your overhead, taxes, and other expenses.

There are many great books and online articles on how to calculate your expenses, set your rates, etc., so I'm not spending time on this here. See Chapter 8 for recommendations. The important thing is to not underprice yourself because you're still stuck in the employee paycheck mentality and feel weird charging a lot more as a consultant.

Note to your future self:
After you have several annual or biannual vision "state-ments" in your archive, go back through your early versions to see how far you've come. Then do something special to celebrate. Splurge on a little catered lunch? Get that fancy pen you're always too cheap to buy? Finally close the office for a week so you can take that vacation to Kabo?
You're the boss.

Pro Tip

Use your roadmapping components to create your marketing plan, client acquisition strategy, or any other guiding documents.

For example:

Your vision could inform your business plan if you want to create one. (I say *want* because I have mixed feelings about business plans for solopreneurs. They have a place and offer value, but the process may prevent you from actually moving forward. Some people fail due to their temperament — always be planning, never be executing, you know what I mean?)

Your vision could also help you set your monthly income goals, so you know what you need to earn each month to bring in the annual revenue you're striving toward.

Your marketing plan could then include specific actions you need to take to achieve your income objectives. How does that monthly number translate into specific types of projects? How many clients or and projects might you need to get there?

Recap

Your Quick To-Do Checklist
for Creating a Roadmap

(At some point) now or later:

✓   Vision statement
✓   Business goals
✓   Income objectives

Don't forget to get your step-by-step cheat sheet with all four components together broken down by tiers at freelancerscompass.com/cheatsheet.

Spotlight on: Kathleen Hackney

Business name: Fayre Marketing
Location: Round Rock, Texas
Founded: August 2023
Business structure: LLC
Website: fayremarketing.com

Kathleen Hackney launched Fayre Marketing after being laid off for the first time in the summer of 2023 and realizing her talents were greatly underutilized in the corporate world. Fayre Marketing provides customer lifecycle marketing strategies and campaigns for small and mid-size businesses.

Kathleen, who has a Master of Business Administration, comes from a corporate career spanning nearly 20 years, including a brief stint in the nonprofit sector. Her background includes working in lifecycle marketing for companies like Cox Communications, Whole Foods Market, and GoDaddy.

What was your biggest challenge when you first got started?

The biggest challenge was understanding the right-sized company and industry that would benefit from my services and be willing to pay for them. At first, I was focused on local small businesses, and it was clear they were not the right fit. In addition, helping these ideal prospects understand the concept and value of customer retention was a hurdle to overcome.

Surprisingly, my niche is very niche — I haven't met any other freelance marketers in my area who offer what I do, so it's been hard to explain how I'm different from the traditional marketing agency.

How did you overcome this challenge, and how long did that take?

After speaking with mentors and other business owners, I determined that I needed to focus my network and marketing efforts on larger companies, starting with those in the Austin, Texas, area since I'm located nearby. I was about four months in when I made this shift from small networking events to larger conferences, business expos, and seminars.

In addition, I started leaning into being a speaker for webinars, workshops, and podcasts to broaden my reach and partner with those who already had a captive audience.

What was your biggest mistake in terms of operations?

I started online advertising right away since it's something I've done in my previous roles. And it produced absolutely nothing. I knew all the best practices, but it was crickets. After a couple of months, I vowed to walk away (although it's hard to walk away from that fun, sexy stuff). I'm competing with Bain Consulting and the McKinseys of the world — I will never have enough budget to match theirs, so it's just not worth the time and money.

What is one thing you wish you knew when you switched from a corporate path?

Most people who shift into freelancing usually start a side hustle while working their full-time gig or they have agency experience, so they know how to navigate being on this side of the fence. I don't have the agency experience to really understand SoWs, account management, business development, pricing proposals, etc.

I've had to fake it till I make it while relying heavily on friends who are already freelancers and consultants. I'm not sure I could have done much more about this fact, but fortunately, I have personal cash on hand for a long runway to figure it out.

How has your business grown, and how did that growth come about?

My business is still young, but my growth has 100% come from networking. I joined the Round Rock Chamber of Commerce and Network In Action (which is a paid networking group), plus I attend several other events in the technology and e-commerce space.

What's your one piece of advice to someone making or contemplating the switch?

You don't have to have your LLC set up or a website or your pricing perfect to begin.

Make a business card and start networking to find out what type of services companies are looking for, what they're willing to pay, and how you could help them. From there, you can build out the right business plan and start building up those other promotional pieces.

What's next for you?

I hope to eventually have enough clients that I'll need to bring on another customer lifecycle marketing strategist. This is such a niche part of marketing, and I'd love to teach someone how to be an expert in retention, loyalty, and revenue growth among a customer base.

PART III

What's Next

With all the basics now in your hands, in this final Part III, I'll leave you with resources and some thoughts on keeping the momentum.

Chapter 7

Keeping the Machine Running

One step, two step.

Small step, big step.

Decisions in the morning, decisions at night.

Decisions that are iffy, decisions that excite.

(With apologies to Dr. Seuss)

As you read in the introduction to this book, the freelance life can be a roller-coaster ride. It doesn't matter how mature your business is, problems outside your control will pop up and make you swear at the universe.

Your biggest client pulls a retainer project. Your bookkeeper quits in the middle of tax season. Your marketing VA ghosts you. ChatGPT steals your job. And on and on.

Even after nearly 25 years in business, I feel hopeless once in a while. Maybe I'm overworked with deadlines, or the economy tanks, or I end up with concurrent projects that drain my emotional energy and make me want to question my life choices.

I don't have a magic potion for these situations that give me the blues. But I do know it helps to ground myself and find the right perspective.

Sometimes that means taking afternoons off to decompress with an art project, sometimes it means venting or moaning to my captive audience (that is, my spouse, my entrepreneurial son, or my Monday buddies), and sometimes it means tapping my coaches, mentors, or peer networks for advice.

It also helps to remember that every less-than-ideal situation is temporary, and I have a lot more control over it than it seems at the surface.

If a retainer client leaves, I can get busy marketing. If the VA disappears, I can give up part of the weekend to recruit a new one and pick up the slack in the meantime. If the economy tanks, I can get a part-time job at McDonald's. Just kidding; I wouldn't make it a day in a fast-food joint — but you get the picture.

One of the best aspects of working for yourself is that you don't have to leave your fate in someone else's hands. Surround yourself with peers, mentors, and other people who can support you, and you'll find a way through.

That being said, if you've tried the freelance life for a while and realized it's not for you, there's no shame in pivoting.

If you're not enjoying what you're doing (for the most part) or can't get past the point of perpetual stress, take your wins — the relationships you made, the personal growth you experienced, the professional experience you gained — and lean on your new strengths as you blaze the next trail.

If, however, you decide to stick it out no matter how rough the ride gets, don't look back.

Imagine where you want your business and career to be in one, three, five years. Create a draft roadmap — and go for it.

One of my favorite quotes is from Jonathan Winters: "I couldn't wait for success, so I went ahead without it." I don't usually stop to think about it, but it's there in one of my email signatures, a subtle, if not subconscious, reminder that if I do the work, the rest will come.

Spotlight on: Nick Vivion

Business name: Ghost Works Communications
Location: Greater Austin, Texas, area
Founded: July 2017
Business structure: LLC
Website: ghost.works

Nick Vivion is a digital nomad whose company offers public relations, brand strategy, and marketing communications for brands in the emerging technology sector. He began his communications career in journalism covering the travel trade, eventually rising to the role of editorial director, managing a team of 12.

When his job was eliminated due to the company's acquisition, Nick decided to start his own content agency for travel and hospitality brands. After losing most of his clients during the pandemic, he pivoted to focus on technology brands and expanded his services.

What was your biggest challenge when you first got started?

The hardest part was managing time and commitments. When you're solo, you're always operating at full capacity, and if a client decides to leave, you don't have a buffer. So it's almost like you're encouraged to always be operating at 110% or 120% just in case someone leaves, and there's a lot of pressure in that.

What is one thing you wish you had considered when you switched from a corporate path?

I definitely was too reluctant to reach out to potential clients because I wasn't sure that people wanted to hear from me. I didn't want to sell, so I didn't do a good job of letting everybody know that

I was launching an agency. I had a couple of clients lined up, which was great, but I should have reached out to all my past contacts in my email and have a real launch. I could have ramped up to 20 clients in six months and gone into growth mode instead of maintenance mode.

What's been the best part of entrepreneurship?

This is not for the faint of heart, but you're in control your own destiny. No matter if you work for yourself or other people, it's still work. But I prefer to be in control of that work and not just have someone fire me one day and leaving me to figure out what to do.

What's your one piece of advice to someone making or contemplating the switch?

Start small to really give it a chance first. I think it's easy to get excited and just quit drastically, but you should test the waters on the weekends and make sure that you really understand what it takes to have a client. Can you get clients and set a bar for how many you'll need to start making, say, $20K as an annual side gig? Set some sort of metric for what you'll need to replace your corporate job and wait until you get to that point. Sure, your life will be insane while you're building such a huge side gig, but you will know that you can have a successful business.

I would try to have some momentum unless you can just convince your former employer to be your first client—and if it's a big enough brand, use that to your advantage. That's a genius move because your former employer saves a lot of overhead when you leave yet you're going to offer them similar services at a lower price. But you have to be careful so they don't expect you to perform exactly like you did as an employee.

I also recommend setting a reasonable time frame to make this work. If in 12 months, for example, you can't make this work, are you going to go back to corporate?

What's next for you?

Business is good, but I'm exhausted working at my current pace, and that's not sustainable for a long time. So, I'm thinking of ways to productize some of my knowledge, especially as I get older. What can I deliver for those who can't afford to pay a PR firm so I can unlock more exponential income?

Chapter 8

A Curated List of Recommended Resources

Don't forget to grab your cheat sheet with a step-by-step checklist of all the operations components — infrastructure, processes, tools and support systems, and roadmap — together, organized by Tier 1–3.

Go to freelancerscompass.com/cheatsheet, where you can also sign up for a 20-minute, complimentary coaching session with me.

Books on Freelancing, Marketing, and Entrepreneurship

Available on amazon.com, etc., unless noted otherwise.

Secrets of Six-Figure Women: Surprising Strategies to Up Your Earnings and Change Your Life by **Barbara Stanny (Huson)**

Although written for women, the advice in this book could apply to anyone. Highly recommended if you need to change your mindset about earning money and embrace a high-earner attitude — and want some strategies for how to get there.

The Freelancer's Bible: Everything You Need to Know to Have the Career of Your Dreams — On Your Terms by **Sara Horowitz, founder of the Freelancers Union**

True to its name, this book provides a comprehensive overview of just about any aspect of a freelancing business, starting with the startup phase and through managing and growing the business. Even after 20-plus years in business, I have found useful advice and ideas I hadn't considered — which supports my earlier point that as a business owner, you're always, always learning.

Worth It: How getting good at the money talk pays off by **Ilise Benun (available at marketing-mentor.com)**

For anyone who doesn't love talking about money (which is almost everyone, in my estimation), this e-book provides scenarios, success stories, pep talks, and more to help you have what Ilise calls "the money conversation." On her website, you'll also find many other great resources, including her *Simplest Marketing Plan*, a toolkit to keep your marketing on track; and *What to Say When*, co-written with Bob Bly, to help you figure out how to respond to clients and prospects in all sorts of situations.

The Freelance Content Marketing Writer: Find Your Perfect Clients, Make Tons of Money and Build a Business You Love by Jennifer Goforth Gregory

Whatever type of services you offer, read this book to get insights into finding clients, negotiating, networking, and other aspects of growing your business. Jennifer also runs a Facebook community (see Digital Communities, below).

Entrepreneurial You: Monetize Your Expertise, Create Multiple Income Streams, and Thrive by Dorie Clark

Read this book after you get your business in a groove and you want to explore other ways you can monetize your knowledge and skills beyond one-on-one client engagements. Dorie spells out a variety of opportunities for creatives, such as coaching, speaking, and podcasting.

Risk Forward: Embrace the Unknown and Unlock Your Hidden Genius by Victoria Labalme

Not technically a book about business, *Risk Forward* is a refreshing — and contrarian — take on how to pivot and embrace the unknown. It's an interesting opposing view of everything we're taught about planning — and it may just work.

Podcasts for Solopreneurs, Freelancers, and Creatives

High-Income Business Writing by Ed Gandia

Not just for business writers, this podcast gives you insights and tips for growing a service-based business. Also check out Ed's website, b2blauncher.com, for a large library of articles on running a business, etc.

Deliberate Freelancer by Melanie Padgett Powers

While a lot of the content is geared toward writers, you'll find honest discussions about the ups and downs of freelancing, along with topics for all business levels.

The Marketing Mentor Podcast by Ilise Benun

As the name implies, this is the podcast about all things marketing, geared specifically to solopreneur creatives.

The BizChix Podcast by Natalie Eckdahl

If you like the idea of having upbeat pep talks combined with no-nonsense advice, check out this podcast from a coach to high-performing women. (This podcast stopped production in May 2024, but with more than 600 episodes, you'll find plenty of content.)

Hidden Brain by Shankar Vedantam

Not exactly about entrepreneurship, this podcast will give you a fun break from thinking about business, along with unexpected takeaways you just might be able to use when working with clients.

Free Professional Advice

SCORE (score.org)

I can't say enough good things about SCORE, which offers free mentorship and advice from both working and retired professionals who specialize in areas like law, accounting, marketing, and e-commerce. There are chapters in each state, but you're not limited to mentors in your location.

When my business was small and I couldn't afford to pay a CPA, lawyer, and marketing coach, I tapped SCORE advisers. I went through the roster of different chapters to handpick people I thought had the right background for me and requested them specifically.

There are limits to what the mentors can advise you on (and you may need to opt for more generic advice if they're outside your state), but you'll get at least a good head start.

Local small business development centers

Check to see if your city, county, or state offers a small business development center. These centers typically offer free resources such as business development advisers and training programs.

I was quite surprised to learn recently that the county next to mine co-sponsors a free business growth program called ScaleUp that includes live virtual meetings for eight weeks, plus a networking platform and other resources that alumni can access in perpetuity.

Local business incubators

Some colleges, universities, and local nonprofits offer business incubator-type programs that provide entrepreneurs with free technical assistance, mentorship, education, and training.

Although many typically focus on larger startups, you may find a local gem that caters to smaller or solo businesses. Some are specifically designed for underrepresented groups, so check into it if that's applicable to you.

Other Websites

The Freelancers Union

Includes a blog with general advice about finances and running a business. freelancersunion.org

Contently

Contently's *The Freelance Creative* blog goes beyond the basics to help freelancers level up. (Alas, Contently, too, stopped publishing new content in May 2024, but the backlog of articles will keep you busy for a while.) contently.net

Copyblogger's blog

While focused primarily on content writing, this blog covers just about any question you might have about freelancing in general. copyblogger.com/blog

Digital Communities

The Freelance Content Marketing Writer group

(An offshoot of Jennifer Goforth Gregory's book)

Facebook: facebook.com/groups/FreelanceCMW

Not just for writers, this is a great place to ask questions and advice about anything related to freelancing.

Superpath

Slack: superpath.co/community

Free membership gives you access to a few channels like freelancing and job listings, while the monthly fee ($20 as of this writing) opens full access to more than a dozen channels where you can ask questions, share insights, and network.

Top of the Funnel

Slack: yesoptimist.com/content-marketing-community

This free Slack community created by the marketing agency Optimist is sort of a digital water cooler for solopreneurs where you can hang out and talk shop, network, learn about running an agency, ask for advice, and more.

Apps and Tools

Project and client management

Trello: My favorite app for keeping track of projects, ideas, resources, tasks, and a lot more. The free option is relatively robust, but I pay for extra functionality. I share some of the Trello boards with my VAs to assign projects.

Asana: A great app if you like lots of bells and whistles, with a free option if you don't need multiple users. I don't use it for my own business, but several of my clients have integrated me into their workflows through Asana. It's a great tool for managing projects that have numerous moving pieces.

Notion: A souped-up variation on Trello, Notion has all the bells and whistles you may want — but too many for me. I felt the learning curve was steeper than what I had patience for. But one of my VAs loves it and set up a shared workspace for us, and I was all for it since I didn't have to figure it out.

Less Annoying CRM: I use this as my marketing CRM, though I know someone who uses it to keep track of projects as well. Less Annoying is quite versatile and customizable, plus super user-friendly. I switched to it from the free version of HubSpot, which was clunky in many ways. Very limited automation and integration are a downside (though emailed reminders are great), plus I would love a better way to segment contact lists.

Time tracking

Clockify: I love Clockify, which is surprisingly robust and reliable for a free app. You can track unlimited clients, projects, and subtasks and run user-friendly reports. There's even a mobile app, which has come in handy for me many times when I was working away from my computer.

Toptal: I used this free app in the past and was surprised that it had excellent email customer support (for a freebie). It has a decent reporting functionality, but the app got glitchy at times. Maybe it's been improved in recent years.

Toggl: I haven't used this personally, but many freelancers I know swear by it.

Communication with clients and your support team

Slack: Unless you're the only lucky knowledge worker on the planet who's never had to use Slack, you likely already know all there's to know about this uber-popular collaboration and communication app (and digital watercooler). I have nothing new to add. I don't love it for client communication personally, but that's because I have so many Slack spaces that I tend to tune out the notifications. That said, it can be useful for sending quick, less formal messages. If you're like me and don't want to live in Slack, simply set boundaries and tell clients what to expect when they communicate with you via the app.

Voxer: Voice memos are not my thing, but some professionals I've worked with love to use Voxer instead of having to type out long messages. Worth a try if you're not the "writing long emails" kind.

Loom: The free version of this video-creation tool is perfect if you want to record your screen for a short explainer. I've used it to walk my VA through the backend of apps or sites before assigning projects like updating my WordPress site.

Signal: If you like texting but want something a little more secure than SMS, this mobile app's for you.

Portfolio Sites

I prefer to use my website for my portfolio because it gives me better control, and there are plenty of plugins (at least for WordPress). But if you need a quick start, below are some options specific to writers.

Note: Some of these are part of freelance platforms that match up freelance writers with gigs, but you can just set up a portfolio without any commitment.

Free: clearvoice.com, contently.com, muckrack.com

Paid but with a limited free version: authory.com, clippings.me, journoportfolio.com

Miscellaneous Information

Setting up your rates

Ilise Benun's *The Creative Professional's Guide to Money* (available on amazon.com) is an older book, but still very relevant. It has several chapters dedicated to setting your rates, plus lots of tips about the money conversation. Also, peruse her resource library at marketing-mentor.com for various pricing-related toolkits you can buy.

Ed Gandia's *Pricing Maximizer toolkit* (available at smarterfreelancing.com/g/egtoolkit/) includes cheat sheets, tips, and more. Also check out Ed's blog at b2blauncher.com for oodles of business tips for solopreneurs — there's an entire category on pricing.

Mindset

Jen Sincero's *You Are a Badass at Making Money: Master the Mindset of Wealth* is a recently discovered gem (thanks, Ed!) that I wish I could have read years (decades!) ago.

It's such an impactful book if you need a new outlook on money (I do, even after all this time) — and even more so if you don't know you need an outlook refresh.

I read this book months after writing the chapter describing how my vision and goals to earn six figures (and to write a book) came to life seemingly out of nowhere — and was vindicated that I didn't just imagine that sometimes the universe works in mysterious ways.

And now we have it on good authority that my idea is not a bunch of hooey. (Well, maybe it still is for you. But humor me and yourself and read this book, if nothing else, for the entertainment factor. Be warned that Jen gets potty-mouthed at times, but that didn't feel like a distraction to me.)

Final Word

"Don't worry about failure. Worry about the chances you miss when you don't even try."

—*Sherman Finesilver*

That's it, my friend. I hope I gave you a lot to think about. If you spend a little time each workweek on these steps, you'll soon be running your operations like a pro.

Once you've implemented your systems, you'll have your business set up for success. That's reason to celebrate! But don't rest on your laurels for long. Your journey as your company's CEO is only beginning.

In the early days, cogs were made out of wood or soft metal and had to be replaced frequently. The technology advanced through the decades, and now cogs are made from much stronger steel alloys. Just like those cogs evolved, so must your business. That means you must always keep an eye on the future, find new ways to improve your skills and your processes, and constantly iterate.

For that to happen, you need the mental space to think about your business, dream up new ideas, and decide how to experiment next.

Give yourself permission — at least sometimes, if not always — to put your business' needs before your clients'. Your business resilience depends on it. All the support systems you're putting in place will improve that resilience and make your business much more successful.

Unfortunately, you can't avoid ups and downs. None of us can.

You can't control outside forces like macroeconomic conditions, technological changes, and so forth. All you can do is prepare the best you can — and avoid growing too comfortable and complacent.

Today, it's ChatGPT. Tomorrow, who knows?

There will always be something new that forces you to re-evaluate your value, business model, and goals. And that's a good thing.

There's nothing like a new problem to jolt you awake, energize you into action, and push you to uplevel once again.

Personally, I recommend being as proactive as you can and anticipate changes. In other words, watch for the writing on the wall and get ahead of the changes as much as possible.

Your future you will thank you.

Acknowledgments

I'm grateful for individuals who have helped my business bloom in recent years and get me to the point of feeling confident enough to share what I know.

First and foremost, my accountability buddies, Diane Faulkner and Mary Rosewood: Words cannot express how invaluable our Monday huddles have been. Your friendship has helped me grow much more than my business. Can you believe we've been doing this for six years? (And I'd be amiss not to mention your patience with my feedback requests for the million iterations of the book title and design!)

Carol Tice, I'm forever in your debt for making accountability buddies part of your Den 2X program, so I could meet these two amazing partners-in-crime. You opened my eyes to all the things I could be doing better in my business, and that was the kick in the pants I needed to up my game. And thank you for keeping us freelancers connected through our Slack community, which is such a powerful resource for any of us otherwise working in a vacuum.

Ilise Benun, your advice, encouragement, and insights are the perfect trifecta for nudging me to get outside of my comfort zone. I deeply appreciate having you to explore the possibilities with me.

Ed Gandia, we've only started working together recently, but I've already learned so much. I've very excited to see where the next chapter takes me with your guidance!

Dee Coppola of Wet Apple Media, you've been an inspiration and a supporter of my career for more than two decades. I can always count on you for suggestions and the right contacts, and I need to thank you more often.

A special thanks to my family: my kids, who had to feed themselves more times than I care to admit and keep themselves occupied while I "always worked"; and my parents, who took care of said kids and much of the household for several years while we squeezed our three-generational family into close quarters. My late father was my role model for an incredible work ethic, and my mother was an inspiration for following my dreams.

I'm also grateful for the professionals who have taken the burden off my shoulders for various aspects of running my business, especially my VAs, Rizza Arendaeng for taking so many time-consuming tasks off my hands and CK Nyakina for lighting the fire under all those branding and marketing efforts.

As for the book, I'm grateful to all the individuals who gave their time to help my dream finally come true.

My early readers — Silvia Klatman, Marsha Hart, and Deborah Stewart — you came through during a time I needed feedback the most, and your suggestions made a huge difference. Nicci Lee, having you as my book accountability buddy truly kept the engine going — without you, I might still be at Chapter 3.

The Tiny Books team, without your "all-you-ever-need-to-know" mother of manuals on book publishing, I probably would have given up because navigating the self-publishing world is not my idea of fun. Your feedback and chapter reviews were just what I needed during the early days. (I'm psyched to see this book in your bookstore soon!)

Mary Rosewood, my copyeditor, I always appreciate your eagle eye. Lucy Arnold, thank you for getting me through the last mile with your design concepts, cover design, and publishing expertise. Karen Zimmerman, your thorough reading of the (almost) final proof saved me from several embarrassing mistakes; I'm in your debt.

And to my small group of friends who offered feedback on the cover design (you know who you are), your ideas and responses made all the difference; a special shout-out to Vanessa McGrady for your subtitle suggestions.

Divya Agrawal, Diane Faulkner, Kathleen Hackney, Amanda Scheldt, Scott Stransky, and Nick Vivion, sharing your experiences and wisdom gives the readers a valuable, expert perspective. Learning from other entrepreneurs about their challenges and wins is one of the best educations possible, and I'm grateful for your generosity.

Last but far from least, to my husband, Darrin.

It's been a long and not always fun roller-coaster ride from those days when you half-jokingly said I should get a "real job." During those times when the fridge and the bank account were both empty, we could not have possibly imagined that one day, I would be in a position to suggest you could take early "retirement" and do your own thing because we really don't need your job. (Yes, selfishly, I just want you there every morning to bring me coffee in bed and around the house during the day when I get hungry.)

You're my rock and my best friend. And although we couldn't be more different, your advice always keeps me grounded. Thanks for supporting me in doing my own thing, letting me drag you along on all those trips you'd rather not take, and indulging all my other crazy whims.

About the Author

Rodika Tollefson is a professional writer and creative with a 25-year career in journalism and marketing. She has run her own business for more than two decades, growing it from a part-time solo gig to a six-figure company.

Throughout her career as a journalist, she has interviewed thousands of small-business owners and leaders about their challenges, strategies, and breakthroughs.

Rodika was on her way to a business major in college when she accidentally discovered she could be paid to write professionally as a journalist. While in the middle of choosing a widget for a "personal selling" assignment in a business class, Rodika realized she was using the wrong skill set and talents to sell ideas. She changed her major to journalism, and the planets finally aligned.

A short stint as a beat reporter steered her toward the freelance writing road. (Who knew a 24/7 reporter's life and small children wouldn't play nice?)

Since then, she has provided writing, editing, content strategy, and graphic design services to clients in the commercial, public, and nonprofit sectors. Her work and leadership have garnered her many accolades, including 40 Under Forty (*Kitsap Peninsula Business Journal*), Purpose-Driven Pen Woman (National League of American Pen Women), and one of 10 Cybersecurity Ghostwriters to Watch (*Cybercrime Magazine*).

Rodika's freelance work has been published in local, regional, national, and international outlets, including *The Washington Post,*

Associated Press, High Country News, Kitsap Sun, The Pen Woman, Dell Technologies Perspectives, Dell Technologies Realize Magazine, and *American Express OPEN Forum/Business Class.* Currently, she works primarily with global technology and cybersecurity enterprises and fast-growing startups. Some of the brands she's worked with include global leading brands such as Cisco, Lenovo, WinZip, Rockwell Automation, and Dashlane.

After all these years, Rodika is still passionate about telling stories — about businesses and the people behind them, and about what makes both of them tick.

Over the past two decades, she has helped hundreds of brands sell their widgets, ideas, and services to the world.

Her business professor would be proud.

Reach Rodika at seattletechnologywriter.com
or freelancerscompass.com.

Did you enjoy *The Freelancer's Compass*?

Help other readers find the book by leaving a review at goodreads.com or at the bookstore website if you purchased it online.

Want to stay in touch and get new articles about all things freelance? Sign up for my email tips at freelancerscompass.com.

And don't forget to grab your cheat sheet (and schedule a complimentary coaching session) at freelancerscompass.com/cheatsheet.

www.ingramcontent.com/pod-product-compliance
Lightning Source LLC
Chambersburg PA
CBHW021458180326
41458CB00051B/6874/J